ON THE
ROAD LESS
TRAVELED

ON THE
ROAD LESS
TRAVELED

An Unlikely Journey from the
Orphanage to the Boardroom

ED HAJIM
WITH GLENN PLASKIN

Skyhorse Publishing

Skyhorse Publishing books may be purchased in bulk at special discounts for sales promotion, corporate gifts, fund-raising, or educational purposes. Special editions can also be created to specifications. For details, contact the Special Sales Department, Skyhorse Publishing, 307 West 36th Street, 11th Floor, New York, NY 10018 or info@skyhorsepublishing.com.

Skyhorse® and Skyhorse Publishing® are registered trademarks of Skyhorse Publishing, Inc.®, a Delaware corporation.

Visit our website at www.skyhorsepublishing.com.

10 9 8 7 6 5 4 3 2 1

Library of Congress Cataloging-in-Publication Data is available on file.

Cover design by Graphique Designs, LLC

Cover images provided by Alamy Stock Photo and Shutterstock.com: ©Andrew Rubtsov/Alamy Stock Photo, ©Susan Law Cain/Shutterstock.com, ©gabczi/Shutterstock.com, ©luchunyu/Shutterstock.com, ©sumroeng chinnapan/Shutterstock.com, ©Rasica/Shutterstock.com

ISBN: 978-1-5107-6424-8
Ebook ISBN: 978-1-5107-6432-3

Printed in the United States of America

To my family—my wonderful wife, Barbara; our three children, G. B., Brad, and Corey; their spouses, Karen, Marthe, and Jim; and our grandchildren, Ra'am, Noam, Luka, Leo, Emma, Sammy, Eddie, and Oscar.

To the University of Rochester and Harvard Business School—for giving me the education that changed my life.

To the United States of America—for giving me the opportunity to realize my dreams.

CONTENTS

Acknowledgments   *ix*

Author's Note   *xvii*

Preface: Two Roads Diverged in a Wood   *xix*

Part 1

1. In Search of the American Dream   3

2. The Kidnapping   13

3. "What Am I Doing Here?   27

4. "Hajim Legs"—Quick and Determined   41

5. Driven to Succeed   49

6. The Ensign and the Engineer   59

7. Business Boot Camp—and Eagles and Gophers   69

Part 2

8. Her Only and Best-Paying Client   81

9. Hit the Go Button   89

10. The Question I Would Have Asked   99

11. Transform or Perish   109

12. The Hornet's Nest   117

13. Greed and Glory   127

14. Egypt, the Galapagos Islands, India, and Beyond!   137

15. Back in Control   145

Part 3

16. A Tale of Two Mergers   153

17. A Suitcase of Letters   161

18. Red Letter Day: August 27, 1997   175

19. Marketus: An Ornery Bear   189

20. The Need to Fix Something   201

21. Coming Full Circle   211

Epilogue: The Four P's—Passion, Principles, Partners, and Plans   217

About the Author   231

ACKNOWLEDGMENTS

THE BOOK THAT YOU'RE ABOUT TO READ is, at its core, all about family. And I could not have written it without mine.

First and foremost, no words suffice for my wonderful wife of fifty-five years, Barbara. She is the heart and soul of our family—my best friend, life partner, the most attentive mother and grandmother imaginable, the true source of my happiness.

Barbara has been patiently involved in the production of this book, contributing her memories, insight, and skills as a researcher, helping me sift through years of our memorabilia, including key letters and some of the vintage photographs featured here.

I also must thank our three children, G. B., Brad, and especially Corey, who encouraged me and worked on and wrote some of the material about my early years.

I must also thank someone who has been an important part of my life for over sixty years—my brother-in-law, David Melnick—as well as his significant other, Marilyn, and their children, Marc and Jennifer. I also lovingly remember my mother-in-law, Mae Melnick (who was like a true mother to me); my father-in-law, Harry Melnick; and Barbara's Aunt Ruth and Uncle Sam.

Also, as you'll see, a secret emerges in this book, and so I am remembering, with great love, my mother, Sophie Hoffman, the gift I found later in life. I must also thank my half brother, Phil, and his wife, Nancy, for being such a key part of my story, too.

As far as the production of this book is concerned, I must thank my editor, bestselling author Glenn Plaskin. His keen insight and editorial abilities were altogether indispensable.

I'm also very grateful to author Laura Morton, who worked closely with me on the groundwork and preliminary drafts of this book, and to former Ogilvy & Mather CEO Ken Roman, who gave me much good advice.

Our book team also included book designer, Michelle Manley, who created the book jacket and interior design, capturing the message of the book with skill and care. Thanks also to our copy editors, Barbara Clark and Penelope Lin.

I must also thank the incredible Lillian Nahas, my "right hand," who has been with me for twenty-six years, successfully taking me through five corporate transitions. I must thank, too, my driver Marty Kelly, who drove me back and forth to Connecticut for sixteen years and over six hundred thousand miles without an accident or a ticket.

On the personal side, among the incredible friends who have been so supportive and to whom I owe so much:

My lifelong friend Rick Safran, a veteran of both orphanages where I lived as a boy, the sharer and keeper of all my early memories; Dick Wedemeyer, my Rochester classmate, navy comrade, Greenwich Management partner, and lifetime friend, always there for me in every possible way; Dr. Zane Burday, who not only helped me when I was at Rochester but also became my physician and confidant for forty years, as I consulted with him on almost everything, physical and otherwise! Other Rochester classmates, close friends for sixty years, include Al "Jesse" James, Sid Shaw, Gene Snyder, Sue Bleyler, Sue Hook, John Gillespie, Gail Papish, Ann Johnson, Jerry Gardner, and Ed Kaplan.

I will always remember, with great fondness, the incredible people I met during my years at Harvard Business School who helped mold my perspective and values in life. They include my study group, Art Bellows, Roger Bullard (my roommate who later lived in Greenwich and was a neighbor for thirty-five years), Jack Nordeman, Jean-Robert Bugnion, and Mal Salter, as well as my HBS golf group, Tony Mayer, Bill Whitman, Bob Burt, Bob Birch, John Hoffman, Jack Nordeman, Charlie Baillie, and Charlie Thomas. Also my good friends Barbara

Franklin and Joan Griewank Colligan, who have been very helpful in making our reunions successful.

A shout-out goes to YPO and CEO forum group members Scoci Scocimara (our leader and a lifelong confidant), Brock Saxe, Bill Lipner, Mort Fuller, Jim Tullis, Bill Morton, Clint McKendrick, Bob Callahan, Ed Carpenter, and Russ MacDonnell. I was privileged enough to draw on their collective wisdom, asking them most of life's questions.

I must acknowledge two investment groups: The Concept Group, founded in 1966 by Mike Steinhardt, myself, and others, later joined by Leon Cooperman; and The Third Thursday Group, which I helped form in 1970. Amazingly, it just celebrated its fiftieth anniversary in the offices of Byron Wien (Vice Chairman of Blackstone's Private Wealth Solutions group), an occasion attended by fellow founders, including Lilia Clemente and Hal Newman, and other original members. Both of these groups have been vital forums for the discussion of trends and ideas.

Among our great family friends who traveled the world with us, I am grateful for Tom O'Malley and his wife, Mary Alice; Charlie and Marilyn Baillie; and Joan and George Schiele.

I also want to thank the incredible neighbors and friends we've known in the communities where we built our lives.

In Greenwich: Lynn Rotando, friend and golf partner for over twenty years, and his wife, Susan; Barbara and John Daly; Kate and Bart Osman; Donna and Henry Clarke; Shelley and Shel Claar; Barbara and Reg Brack; Debbie and Asa Davis; Mike Gellert; John Hill Wilson; Nancy and Ron Lynch; Chris and Jim Cowperthwait; Harley and Steve Osman; Art and Jody Bellows; Lynn Glenn; Marsha Berger; Regina and George Rich; Randi and Fred Filoon; and Jane and Alan Batkin.

In New York: Barbara and Peter Georgescu, as Peter's life and books were an inspiration for this book; the incredible Nancy Lieberman, fellow board member of both the University of Rochester and the River House; our cousin Madalyn and her husband Hal Rosenbluth; New York and Nantucket neighbors Carolyn and Ian Mackenzie; our cousins

Carol and Dan Mastropietro; and Charlie Hess, who has been a great help to me for decades.

In Ocean Reef, now our primary residence: Barbara and Emery Olcott, Bessie and John Connelly, Nancy and Ron Harrington, Cynthia and Patrick Lee, Sally and Tom Davidson, Barbara and Paul Ferri, Stevie and Marshall Wishnack, Judy and Rick Brand, Lowell and Luisa Bryan, Bill and Nancy McPherson, Connie and John Taylor, Margo and Rich Miller, and Karen and T. J. LeTarte.

Nantucket has been our summer sanctuary for the past thirty-five years. It would impossible to list all the wonderful people who have touched our lives there, including our colleagues on the boards of the Nantucket Historical Association and the Nantucket Conservation Foundation, the members and staff of the Nantucket Golf Club, with special thanks to Tommy Bresette and Kathy Costa. I can't forget my Friday breakfast group, the "Doomsday Boys," Mark Sandler, Nick Nicholas, Charles Hale, Mike Campbell, Ken Richardson, and Tom Anathan.

Among my mentors, I give heartfelt thanks to Reuben Koftoff, the "Boss" at the Hebrew National Orphan Home who helped me at a very critical time; Oscar Minor, the professor at the University of Rochester who got me through mechanical drawing and served as counselor on my extracurricular activities; Dr. Su, my chemical engineering professor and senior project supervisor; Navy Commander Charles C. Gibson, who counseled me throughout my naval service and wrote the recommendation that must have gotten me into Harvard Business School; and Deans Kim Clark, Jay Light, and Nitin Nohria, Professors Uyterhoeven, Hunt, and Law of HBS, and Sol Gittleman of Tufts University. Among the brilliant writers who have inspired me: first, special thanks to my friend Howard Stevenson, author of *Just Enough*, a book filled with incredible wisdom. Four other writers who have played an important part in shaping my perspective on life: Daniel Levinson of *The Seasons of a Man's Life*; John Wooden of *Pyramid of Success*; Lou Holtz of *Three Rules for Living a Good Life*; and Harvey Mackay, author of many inspirational books. The Four P's philosophy that you will read about in the Appendix of this book was inspired by the writings of these five people.

Special thanks also go to Jim Fullerton, chairman of Capital Research, who guided me through all of my career; Bob Egelston, president of Capital Research, who taught me the business of investing and supported me in my first venture; Wally Stern, a friend and Wall Street legend who always made time for me; Bob Fomon, president and CEO of E. F. Hutton; and Pete Peterson, chairman and CEO of Lehman Brothers, who set an example of how to manage people fairly.

Among my great colleagues, I must mention: Steve Blecher, an invaluable friend and partner who worked with me for thirty years and did everything I did not want to do or could not do—and did it all brilliantly!—and Mike Sherman, who became my partner at Hutton and Lehman and shared so many of his insights on the market and the world; Steve Reynolds, my partner at Greenwich Management; as well as Steven Spiegel, my friend and confidant who helped me transform the image of Lehman Securities.

I will always be grateful to the founders of Furman Selz, Roy Furman and Bernard Selz, who sought me out and gave me a chance to build a company. Also at Furman Selz were my great colleagues: Brian Friedman, who built our banking business; Bill Shutzer, who took our banking business up to a whole new level; Rob Watson and Bob Lyster, who managed sales and research at Furman Selz; and Bill Turchyn, who was a prime mover in our asset management group.

On the academic board side of things, I want to thank Christine Fairchild, associate dean of external relations at Harvard Business School, who enlisted me on the board of the HBS Alumni Association; and Susan Good, who followed me as president of the Alumni Association board.

I'm grateful to Joel Seligman, president of the University of Rochester, whose leadership and drive created an inflection point in the university's history. As chairman of the board of trustees, I was honored by Joel's generosity in erecting a statue of me on the Hajim School of Engineering and Applied Sciences Quadrangle. And heartfelt thanks go to Richard Feldman, who took over as interim president of the University of Rochester and brought things back to an even keel; and the late, great Paul Burgett, dean and vice president at the University of Rochester, a very special supporter and friend, and one of Rochester's most prominent and beloved figures. I also must thank Mark Taubman, the CEO of the Medical Center; Rob Clark, the university's provost and past dean of the Hajim School of Engineering and Applied Sciences, who raised its quality while tripling its enrollment; and Mark Zupan, past dean of the Simon Business School, for his help and guidance during my time as chairman of the board of trustees.

I also want to thank Lamar Murphy, general secretary to the Rochester board, and Gail Norris, the general counsel, who was instrumental during the years I was a trustee and chairman of the board of the University of Rochester. I must also thank Steve Milne, a Rochester University safety officer. For more than a decade, during my seventy trips to the University, Steve made sure that I got to every one of my appointments on time!

I thank Jim Thompson, senior vice president of development at the University of Rochester, along with Jack Kreckel for their outstanding work in helping me to construct my gift to the university; his successor, Tom Farrell and his right hand Erin Moyer for completing our record-setting capital campaign; and Marty Messinger, whose example as a trustee and philanthropist is unmatched.

There are so many people at the university that I wish to thank, including the more than sixty trustees. I want to give special thanks to Bob Witmer, Bob Goergen, Danny Wegman, Rich Handler, Tom Sloan, Larry Bloch, Gail Lione, Nomi Bergman, Gwen Greene, Bernie Ferrari, Lance Drummond, Kathy Murray, Carol Karp, Cathy Minehan, Larry Kessler, Nat Wisch, and so many others.

A final note for Rochester: Sarah Walters was one of the first Hajim Scholars and I'm so proud of her success in achieving a PhD in optical engineering. In her achievement, she has given me a special gift.

On a personal note, I want to express heartfelt thanks to my two physicians, Alan Lebowitz and Rebecca Kurth, and to my longtime physical therapists, Eveline Erni and Janna Fournier.

Finally, thanks to my stimulating friend André Perold, whom I have known since my Lehman days, and who asked me to chair his company at my current advanced age! I also want to thank my three young partners for allowing me to be involved in their businesses: Brett Keith of Rockwood Equity, Bob Israel of One Stone Partners, and Ross Koller of Koller Capital. And a big thanks to Jason Trennert, Ted Fischer, and Saad Alam for including me in their ventures.

And now, with all those thanks, off to the story!

Ed Hajim
(September 2020)

AUTHOR'S NOTE

A S I SIT HERE IN THE SUMMER of 2020, the world is grappling with several challenges, one of which is a collective questioning of how the world works. I have always believed in the American dream because I lived it, but I recognize that for some that dream has not been within reach for reasons that we should acknowledge.

I started to consider sharing my story about a decade ago when the length of my life began to outpace the time that was left. I hope there are lessons and inspiration within these pages that can help people get past obstacles they face.

I have always appreciated the tremendous role luck played in my life story, and that's why I have made it my mission to give back. Wealth is a tricky subject. I was born without family or financial support and as result, both became important to me. I knew money could mean more freedom and opportunity, for me and for my children.

For those of us who have been fortunate, our responsibility is to make sure that everyone has the opportunity to join our ranks and to continue the cycle of helping others so that someday no one will be left behind.

Life is about continuous learning. There can be a tension between the wisdom you gain along a life's journey and the change around you. I have always believed I could keep learning and try to be a better person. My kids used to make fun of the high stack of self-help books on my bed stand.

I also believe that when the student is ready the teacher appears. The pandemic may seem like an unlikely teacher, but it has given us a lot to think about. I have tried to listen to its lessons. It's difficult, but the journey is never complete. And that is what makes the road we travel more interesting.

Peace,
Ed Hajim

Two Roads Diverged in a Wood

L IFE CAN BE TOUGH, filled with frustration, pain, and all kinds of heartache. It often starts in childhood—as it did for me. And I'm not alone.

All kids depend upon adults to protect and love them, but it doesn't always happen that way. My parents both loved me. *They did.* But as you'll read in the following pages, love isn't always enough to create a home.

There are many kids out there who are neglected, abandoned, and abused. But even when faced with adversity, some children persevere and succeed, overcoming hardship to accomplish great things, while others sink into misfortune, unable to conquer their pain or improve their circumstances.

What makes the difference? Put two people in identical circumstances, and one rises to the top while the other sinks, feeling victimized by the past.

I was one of those kids who had a tough start, separated from my mother at the age of three and raised in foster homes and orphanages. I felt incredibly lonely and abandoned—and later astonished by a family secret I didn't discover until the age of sixty.

But I enjoyed a successful career in the financial world, building a happy, prosperous life along the way. I often wonder how I did it. Despite the difficult start, what drove me? What drives anyone to succeed regardless of childhood circumstances?

Personal happiness and financial success aren't accidental. Nor are they a matter of predetermined fate. Talent isn't the most important element, either, because everyone has talent, though not everyone mines and develops it.

The answer is that several factors combine to create success and happiness. In my case, the adversity I experienced as a kid made me self-reliant, and in turn gave me an unshakable self-confidence. When you have to do things by yourself, you just do.

I also had an intense hunger for financial security. In my childhood, the perfect life that I saw depicted on the silver screen, with lots of family love and abundance, didn't exist. Unlike a kid who has everything and wants for nothing, I was hungry. I was hungry for everything. I had to fight against the current and pull myself forward through my own efforts, because there was nobody there to help me, nobody to give me financial support or a head start.

Honestly, that hunger was a gift that kept on giving throughout my life, leading me to explore, to contribute, and finally to give to others the very thing I had never had myself. I would later come to believe that the resources we need to turn our dreams into reality are within us, waiting for the day we decide to wake up and claim them.

I woke up at an early age. But not everyone has that epiphany. I also had some lucky breaks, which in the late 1940s and early 1950s weren't easy to come by for a person without resources to start with.

In the end, adversity is a gift. If you don't experience it, you'll never know how to overcome it. The disadvantages I endured sparked my ambition and work ethic. So it wasn't fate. It was drive—some call it grit. It's the one thing privileged people who feel entitled to everything and have nothing to fight for often lack. That was never me.

You have to have a dream. You have to develop values to live by. You have to have discipline and the desire to improve your circumstances.

You have to have a willingness to work for what you want in life. And, of course, a little luck never hurts! It's essential.

All along the way, I've made pivotal decisions that changed the entire course of my life. Many of them entailed significant risk. But we all have moments when we face a decision that will make all the difference. It reminds me of one of my favorite poems by Robert Frost, "The Road Not Taken."

> *Two roads diverged in a yellow wood,*
> *And sorry I could not travel both*
> . . . .
> *I took the one less traveled by,*
> *And that has made all the difference.*

That's so true for me. I have always moved down new roads, asking myself which direction to go in for more exposure to things that challenge me. I pushed the envelope in order to discover potential interests and limits. As you'll read, it became a lifelong pattern of doing the unexpected and reaching higher, testing myself whenever I could. As a high school freshman, I took Latin, an upper-class course that I nearly flunked. Oh well.

As a senior in high school, I took spherical geometry, attempted by few and not conquered by me.

As a sophomore in college, I took physicists' physics rather than the required engineers' physics. I got a D plus. And on it goes. But I was game to try anything.

Since I was in my forties, as I faced key life decisions, I often reread M. Scott Peck's classic book *The Road Less Traveled*, published in 1978, and I've tried to apply many of his principles.

For example, Peck commends the value of delaying gratification and keeping an eye on the future. Sensing the wisdom of this, I often put off something that might have been easy or pleasurable to accomplish in favor of a more important long-term goal. (I think of the time I went to business school when I could have saved my money and enjoyed the life of a successful engineer.)

Peck also advocates accepting responsibility, being dedicated to the truth, balancing your life, and facing the need to work out your difficulties: "Life is full of problems," he writes. "We can moan about them, or we can solve them." Throughout my life, I have gotten great joy out of trying to solve them. At times, my survival depended upon it. I especially like Peck's definition of love, which is *giving* to others—to yourself, to your family, to your work, and to your community, something I have tried to do all my life.

He finally writes of the power of grace, which is a gift, a spiritual healing that comes to us without our seeking it. I do believe that there is a higher power that has favored me throughout my life. Otherwise I would never have been able to do many of the things you'll read about in this book.

As I look back, I can see how every person who crossed my path led me toward success—my foster parents, my teachers, other orphaned boys, my professors, my college friends, a navy captain, my business partners, my wife, my children, and many others. Each relationship presented an experience that drove me down the road that would become the pathway of my life.

I was lucky to meet these people. They all played a hugely important role in what happened to me. And for that, I'm profoundly grateful.

Likewise, I've always wanted to be an important person in *other* people's lives—I want others to know that I am there to help them realize their dreams. I hope what you read in the pages ahead will inspire you to fight for your dreams and to dare to do the unconventional, to travel down the road less taken.

Here's my story.

PART ONE

In the Beginning

My father, Jack, with the single-propeller plane he owned (1928)

CHAPTER ONE

In Search of the American Dream

c. 1936–1939

APRIL 2015: It was a perfect spring day in Washington, DC—the kind every local chamber of commerce dreams about. The cherry trees were in full bloom, and their fragrance filled the air. The sun shone high overhead in a cloudless, vibrant blue sky.

There I was in our nation's capital with my family to receive the Horatio Alger Award, which honors American leaders who have accomplished successes in spite of adversity, proving, as the Horatio Alger Association's motto goes, that "hard work, honesty and determination can conquer all obstacles."

After the induction ceremony that night, I would become one of the seven hundred people who had been recognized over the past seventy-plus years. And though I was deeply and profoundly honored by it, I was also a little nervous.

With a few hours to spare before the evening festivities began, I wanted to escape the confines of our hotel and get some fresh air. I asked my wife, Barbara, if she'd like to take a walk to the Smithsonian to see the history of transportation exhibition that was on display at the time. She knew I was getting a bit anxious about the event and that this would be a good outlet for me. You see, I have a hard time sitting still under the best of circumstances, and the idea of my most private and personal childhood stories going public at the awards ceremony was making me increasingly uncomfortable.

"A walk might do you some good, Ed," Barbara said sympathetically.

No one knows me better than my wife, my partner of more than fifty years, so off we went.

But as we entered the exhibition room, I stood shell-shocked, frozen in time. There, right in front of us, was a 1930s Ford roadster and, behind it, a large map of the western United States. A long black line on the map traced the path of Route 66 from St. Louis to Los Angeles.

I didn't say a word.

I took a long, deep breath, closed my eyes, and suddenly I was three years old again, traveling that same route in a similar car with my father, who had just kidnapped me from my mother.

THE ROOTS OF THAT DAY in the Smithsonian go all the way back to the turn of the last century, to the origins of the Hajims in the Middle East. According to my father, he was descended from a long line of Syrian Jewish metals traders. In order to conduct their business, his grandparents traveled by camel train back and forth between Iran and France. As a result, he, his parents, and his grandparents were fluent in Farsi and many other languages, including Arabic and Hebrew.

In the 1890s, during one of these trips, my great-grandfather was mysteriously murdered near Aleppo, Syria. I suspect the fact that they traded in gold, among other metals, had something to do with it. In any case, this event caused my father's grandmother—my great-grandmother, who was reportedly a very strong woman—to make the decision to take the family to the New World.

The clan arrived in New York City in 1900. At the time, my grandmother was pregnant with my father. I don't know if he was born in Aleppo, on the boat coming over, or in New York, but he somehow ended up with two birth certificates. One shows that he was born in Aleppo, and the other shows that he was born in Manhattan. The former shows the name Jack S. Adjme. I later discovered that the *S* stands for Sassoon—a name he might have made up so he could associate himself with the Sassoon family, known as the Rothschilds of the East, though I don't think we are related.

When the group disembarked at Ellis Island, the immigration officials couldn't pronounce or spell Adjme (in English, the closest you can come is ADJ-mee), so somehow the name was altered to Hajim, pronounced HAY-jim. Like those of so many other families, my last name is something of an immigration accident, created on the spot as a matter of convenience by someone unrelated to the family.

At the time, there was an enclave of Syrian Jews living in Bensonhurst, Brooklyn, so my family settled in among that community. According to my father, he was the only son for a fourth generation in his family—making me the fifth such individual. But that turned out not to be true, because he had a brother. My father always did love to tell a good story.

THE SYRIAN JEWISH COMMUNITY in Bensonhurst was tightly knit, and my father's mother and grandmother were prominent figures within it. My paternal grandfather, though amiable, wasn't financially successful. Regardless, my father seemed to do well in high school. He became fascinated with radio, a new technology for that day and age, and I have a picture of him with a group of his classmates that was published in the *New York Times*. The students are posed around a radio, rabbit ears prominently on display. My father also apparently enjoyed athletics and became a track star while he was in high school.

By the time my father graduated, at the age of eighteen, he had taken a few technical courses and subsequently went to work for RCA. I think it always bothered him that he never earned a college degree, because he was an extremely intelligent man who placed a high value on the importance of getting an education. In fact, he considered it a privilege. He told me that while he was working at RCA, he was on the team that helped invent the low-frequency radio antenna. I don't know what his role in or contribution to the effort was—or even if the story is true—but my father beamed with pride whenever he spoke of those days. I believe it was the only time in his life when he was truly happy. That period of stability ended on Black Tuesday—October 29, 1929—which robbed my father of everything he had. Like so many American investors, he was caught by surprise, and the stock market crash effectively wiped out his assets overnight, destroying his spirit in the process. Until that fateful day, my father had become quite successful, having accumulated enough capital to own his own home. He also had a strong portfolio of investments, with quite a bit of equity in RCA. He supposedly had real estate holdings in New York City, too, including buildings on 110th Street and a shooting gallery in Coney Island that he had bought for his own father. I even have a picture of my father standing next to a small propeller-driven airplane that he owned. All in all, he appeared to be well on his way to becoming a very wealthy man. However, my father, like millions of others, wasn't financially prepared for the downfall of the market and took the sudden and shocking economic downturn very hard. He had bought his stock in RCA on margin, which means that he borrowed money in order to make the investment. In the 1920s, one was allowed to borrow as much as 90 percent of the value of the stock—which was what he did. In that situation, even a small change in the market can wipe out an investment, and with the severe drop in prices, my father was in a very bad position. To survive, and to repay his creditors, he was forced to liquidate everything.

Although the ensuing years were challenging for all Americans, for my father the crash was a devastating blow from which he would never recover. Unfortunately, despite his efforts to reestablish himself as the businessman he once was, that dream would elude him for the rest of his days.

By 1933, my grandmother had died, and my grandfather had lost the shooting gallery my father had bought for him. With all his money gone, my father was left with only one thing of value—his car, which in his mind offered a means of escape. Destitute, and facing what he thought were his only two choices—suicide or migration to the other side of the country—my father decided to leave his beloved New York City behind. He headed to California in pursuit of steady work, renewed riches, and professional success, the three things he longed for but would never have again.

Thus he packed his car and drove west, toward the land of promise and a new beginning. His first stop was St. Louis, where he visited a distant cousin by the name of Levin. Given the difficulty of the times, this relative was not particularly welcoming. He had six children, the second youngest of whom was a beautiful eighteen-year-old girl named Sophie.

Sophie's family life was not a happy one. Her parents, Jews of Eastern European descent, owned a dry goods shop, where they bought and sold inexpensive clothing. Sophie, along with her siblings, worked in the shop, though she wasn't close to any of her brothers and sisters. Why? I don't really know the specifics of the family dysfunction. But it might have had something to do with the hardships of growing up in a large family when financial resources were scarce.

My father stayed with the family for two weeks. During this time, against all odds, he and Sophie developed a mutual attraction. At the age of thirty-three, the last thing my father expected was to fall in love with a girl fifteen years his junior, but that's what happened.

Sophie instantly fell for my father. She saw him as an exotic, dashing stranger who had come to sweep her off her feet. She also saw an opportunity: he offered a means of escape from her straitened circumstances and her unhappy home life. To her, Jack Hajim was attractive, well groomed, told a good story, and owned his own car. What else could she want? These were all desirable qualities in a man back then. Two short weeks after my father arrived in St. Louis, much to the dismay of everyone else in the Levin family, Jack and Sophie were married! And then they drove away to Southern California to start a new life in search of the American dream.

UNFORTUNATELY, it soon became evident that the cross-country move to Los Angeles didn't help my father's career prospects. Employment was hard to come by, as was any hope for a steady paycheck. Still, my dad had taken the federal civil service exam and received a high grade. This qualified him for jobs at electrical plants, but somehow, even when he did manage to land these jobs, they never lasted very long.

My father claimed that both his difficulty in getting hired and his frequent dismissals resulted from the fact that he was Jewish. He complained bitterly about anti-Semitism and believed that it prevented him from getting the jobs he deserved. In my view, he couldn't stop seeing himself as a victim. Yes, anti-Semitism probably played some part in his problems, but he was using it as an excuse to cover up his shortcomings as a provider. (He was also ignoring the obvious—that his personality clashed with anyone in authority.)

In 1935, my father suffered another blow when my grandfather was hit by a truck and killed. My father always maintained that the driver was drunk at the time, and in his later years my father would still get angry when he spoke of that driver.

The one blessing in my parents' life, or so I've been told, came early in the marriage, in 1936, when they welcomed me into their loving arms at the Queen of Angels Catholic hospital in Los Angeles. But the joy of being new parents quickly wore off when the reality of having another responsibility—a big, crying one—became painfully clear. There was my mother, a twenty-one-year-old homemaker, and my father, a frustrated out-of-work technician, both inexperienced as parents and overwhelmed by the responsibility of a baby. Without financial resources, they often argued and were quite stressed. All this began to take its toll on their relationship.

Compounding the economic problems was the fact that my father ruled the household as if he were a monarch. He was like the despotic character Ibrahim in the novel *The Haj* by Leon Uris: the undisputed head of the household. His attitude was "It's my way or the highway."

He treated my mother like a servant in many ways. He wouldn't allow her to work and help support the family, even though her earnings would certainly have helped him. I think he felt ashamed of his financial condition.

He was also very set in his ways, which made him rigid and demanding. He had rather unusual eating habits, too, something my mother would have known if they had properly courted before marrying. He was a strict vegetarian and wanted her to cook exclusively meat-free meals for him. This doesn't seem unusual today, but it was quite out of the ordinary at the time. In addition, my eccentric father was strict about his appearance, especially when it came to cleanliness. You might say he was obsessive about it.

To make matters worse, he was subject to unpredictable bursts of anger. I can attest to that: I have a memory of being two or three years old and my parents arguing as they stood by my crib. My father took hold of the crib by the railings and shook it. Although in later years my mother said that didn't happen, it was certainly true that all he had to do to make me cry was look at me.

Growing ever more desperate to support his family, my father had no choice but to start taking whatever work he could find—wherever he could find it. As a result, he bounced around from job to job, moving my mother and me from Los Angeles to small towns all over the country. At one point, over my mother's objections, we moved to Atlanta, Georgia. During these sojourns, we usually lived like gypsies in motel rooms. Yet no matter how hard he tried, my father never found a long-term position—or even the promise of one.

It seemed almost impossible to believe: he was the kind of man who could take a radio apart and put it back together again. He repaired things with ease and precision. Yet he wasn't able to apply his talents in a meaningful or substantive way, and he was never able to secure full-time employment or create a safe and secure home life for my mother and me.

My mom was young and naive and didn't know how to deal with my father's depression over the desperate state of family affairs. She was a smart and kind woman, perhaps a bit too passive. But how could she possibly understand the demons haunting her husband when even he didn't?

My mother didn't have any idea what she had gotten herself into when they married. Between his stormy moods, his irritability, and his regimented personal habits, my father was a handful, and she had no way to cope with him.

By 1939, relations between my parents had become extremely strained. These were tough times for a lot of families, especially in the aftermath of yet another down market in 1937 and in a world that was facing war and recession. Ultimately, the combination of my father's overbearing personality and their unsettled lifestyle had simply become too burdensome for my mother to tolerate. Feeling as if she had no other imaginable recourse, she filed for divorce and full custody of her son and was granted both. And then, with no place else to go, my mother and I went back to St. Louis to start a new life together.

My dad and me (1938)

CHAPTER TWO

The Kidnapping

c. 1939–1946

MY MOTHER AND I had no place to go except back to her family home, which was not ideal. The family was struggling financially. Upon our arrival, her father wasn't very happy to see either his daughter or a three-year-old child! To him, it meant two more mouths to feed.

In addition, divorce was fairly rare in that era, and I think my grandfather disapproved of what my mother had done in the wake of her six-year marriage. Yes, it took a tremendous amount of courage to strike out on one's own as a single mother. But other people might not have seen my mother's decision in a positive light. In fact, they might have looked down on her as a scorned woman.

Life in St. Louis was simple and stable, but there's at least some evidence that my mother had trouble taking care of me. The few photos I've seen from that time show me unkempt, with a dirty face. I was only a toddler, so I don't have any true recollections of the way things really were. Still, it must have been emotionally difficult for my mother to live in a place that didn't feel welcoming.

My father was ordered to pay five dollars a week in alimony and child support and was granted visiting rights on Sundays. But it was obviously impossible for him to visit every Sunday, because it required a drive of more than eighteen hundred miles along Route 66 each time. So after his first visit, it was several months before I would see him again.

One Sunday late in 1939, my father arrived in St. Louis as expected for his scheduled second visit. He picked me up in his car, his Ford roadster, as he had done the first time, but instead of taking me to the playground or out to lunch, he just kept driving. He sailed onto Route 66, stepped on the gas pedal, and headed west. Though I was too young to understand, once we were safely out of St. Louis, my father turned to me and said, "Eddie, we're going to Los Angeles." He said I was better off with him than with my mother.

———————

I NEED TO PAUSE HERE, because that single event profoundly shaped the course of my life, perhaps more than any other. Talk about a road less traveled! My father had driven me down a road that I did not choose, so I had no control over what would happen next. At the time, at the age of three, I wasn't sure what to say, so I just sat in silence. All I could do was press my cheek against the cool glass, stare out the window, and watch as the other cars on the highway whizzed by.

But in the years to come, I would view this as what it was—a kidnapping.

Malcolm Gladwell, in his book *David and Goliath*, argues that a person's disadvantages can sometimes work to his or her advantage. (In fact, he goes further to suggest that there is a category of people called *eminent orphans*—successful individuals who have lost a parent early in life, often before the age of ten.) I've come to believe this is true: if I hadn't suffered the hardships I was subjected to as a child—the worst of which were yet to come on that day in 1939—I wouldn't have had the success I enjoy today.

Ever since I was a young child, I envisioned my life's journey as a narrow mountain road that dropped off steeply on either side. There were no guardrails to prevent me from plunging into the canyons below. There was little margin for error.

To the left was the canyon called poverty. I didn't want that in my future.

To the right was the canyon I'll call failure. I didn't want that in my future, either! Staying in the middle of the path was hard: every misstep—a bad grade, a wrong decision, a poor choice—made it all the more likely that I would fall off the road.

On that day in 1939, I was at the beginning of the road—a kind of Route 66 of my imagination. I may not have been conscious of it at the time, but that was when I began to perceive those canyons on either side of me.

My father's actions changed the course of my life forever. From my perspective now, his decision to literally kidnap me was outrageous. But one thing was clear to me at the outset and remains clear to me to this day: he must have loved me very much to do what he did. I believe he found the separation from me unbearable, knowing that I was eighteen hundred miles away in St. Louis.

I also believe he might honestly have thought he could take better care of me than my mother could, especially if he saw that my face was dirty and my clothes unclean. Perhaps there was an element of revenge against my mother, too, because she had sole legal custody of me, a fact that must have irked him. So he followed the only course of action *he* thought was open to him: he took me away.

THE TRIP FROM ST. LOUIS TO LOS ANGELES took several days. We stopped along the way at modest roadside motels, most of which wouldn't accept small children, so I had to stay in the car until my father could sign for the room. Then he'd hide me under his big overcoat and sneak me inside. I remember him saying I was so little that I could practically fit in the coat's inside pocket. I was scared and wondering why I couldn't just hold my father's hand, as other kids did.

After we had lived in Los Angeles for a short time, he said my mother died and I would not see her again. Being only three at the time, I don't remember reacting to the news, nor can I recall how it affected me. I don't think I cried, because I didn't understand what it meant. I was just a little kid. What did I know? I had no reason to doubt him.

For the first few months, my father and I lived in a series of small, inexpensive hotels around Los Angeles. He'd put me to sleep, then slip off to the lobby to smoke a cigar. Sometimes I would get up and go downstairs to beg him to come back to our room. He was all I had, and I hated waking up and finding him gone. My dependence on him was absolute.

In those early days, my father frequently told me he loved me more than anything else in the world. To a three-year-old who had just lost his mother, it seemed like pure, unconditional love. He could be gruff, yes, but he was physically demonstrative and hugged me often. Nonetheless, I was obviously a bigger burden than he expected. Why? Because nine months after he and I arrived in Los Angeles—shortly after I turned four—I found myself living with a Mrs. Benson, a neighbor we'd met in our travels. It seemed my father had gone to work as a radio operator on a merchant ship and shipped off to Australia, leaving me behind.

By late 1940, with the challenges of the Great Depression finally easing, my father was able to return to California and get himself back on track again, at least for a while. Using some of the money he had saved through hard work and frugal living, he purchased a couple of small tuna fishing boats and manned them with a team of experienced immigrant Japanese fishermen. I have wonderful pictures of my father and me on those boats.

For a short period, life felt normal. I had come back from living with Mrs. Benson and was living with my father. He and I were buddies: we took trips to the desert and spent time together playing at the beach. He took me on pony rides and to the Santa Monica Pier. It was idyllic in a way.

Still, I often felt flashes of his temper, which could erupt at any moment. I have one memory of him carrying me through Los Angeles City Hall, yelling and screaming at people as he went. I was crying up a storm. Later I read in the newspaper that he had called a prosecutor in court a liar. I can only surmise that he was having a conflict with his employer, possibly because he felt he was a victim of anti-Semitism. Whatever the reason, my father seemed to have ugly arguments with just about everybody.

Nonetheless, things seemed to be going well until the bombing of Pearl Harbor and America's entry into World War II. In a matter of weeks, the all-Japanese crews on my father's fishing boats were interned in heavily guarded camps, and his small business quickly fell apart.

Once again, my father was left with next to nothing. Feeling desperate and with no place to turn, in 1942 he became a lieutenant in the United States Merchant Marine. As a radio operator, he was one of three or four senior officers aboard the vessel. He told me he'd been called into the service because of his knowledge of the US West Coast waters and because of his highly specialized radio communications skills.

Of course, I was too young to know that there were few, if any, forty-one-year-old single parents being drafted at the time. I believe he volunteered—parenthood had proved too much for him to handle. So even though I was denied a mother, he made the decision to leave. And he was almost immediately sent to sea.

I have to say that it was a sad, dark day when my father left me for the second time, and it marked the beginning of my life in a series of foster homes. He had called a Catholic welfare agency and explained that he *had* to go to sea. He told the agency that I had no mother and asked if they would get me into the foster care system as soon as possible. The agency, of course, had no idea that my father was lying to intentionally keep me away from my mother, a cruel strategy that it wouldn't have tolerated had the agency known about it. In any case, the agency quickly placed me with a family that neither my father nor I had ever met, strangers to us both.

I'll never forget the horrendous day he dropped me off.

Gasping for air, I cried out for him, begging him not to leave me behind. "Why? Why are you doing this? I'll be a good boy. I won't be a problem. Please, Daddy. Don't leave me." Like any child, I blamed myself. I just couldn't otherwise understand his decision to abandon me. Why would any parent do this?

I cried so hard that I actually threw up. But my tears and pleas weren't enough to make him stay.

So I stood there, alone, and watched my father slowly walk away without even turning around or looking back. Perhaps it was his guilt, or his own sadness, that made him act that way. I fell to my knees and quietly whimpered as his slim, dark figure faded into the horizon and then was gone from my sight. It was the worst thing I'd ever experienced. As I perceived it, *that* was the day I lost the only family I had in the world. But leaving me was the only way he could make a living—or at least that's what he must have told himself.

THE FIRST FOSTER HOME I lived in was awful. The family was only in it for the money from the agency, and wasn't interested in me at all. There was no love, no warmth. Instead, there was physical violence in the household. The father had a strap he used to thrash me with. He would take me to a shed in the back of the property and use it freely. The Catholic social worker, Miss Rush, would come to the house once every couple of months, but there was no way I could tell her what was going on.

Life in that house was cold, distant, and lonely. I was also scared, always afraid that I would say or do something that would lead to getting beaten again. At this point, I was also beginning to become aware of my anger. Even at the age of six, I must have realized, on some deeply buried level, that I could use my anger as a weapon and lash out at the people who I believed were mistreating me.

The family enrolled me in Catholic school, and though I received some good grades, this was the start of a phase in which I misbehaved and rebelled against any and all authority figures. The nuns considered me very mischievous and not easy to handle, and I did my best to reinforce that impression.

It was during my time in the second foster home that the Catholic welfare agency discovered I wasn't Catholic. I don't know how it found out, but my Jewishness was a problem: the agency's services were intended for Catholic children only. I suspect that despite this, what kept me in its good graces, and eligible to receive its services, was that the agency knew I had been born in a Catholic hospital.

My father was an expert at concealing our Jewishness from anyone he thought might use it against us. Indeed, that's why he wanted me to be born at Queen of Angels Hospital. As he explained it, he felt that Catholic hospitals were cleaner and better run than other facilities.

But shortly after my birth, when it was time to have me circumcised, the Catholic nurses and doctors were taken aback: they didn't perform that operation at their hospital. Somehow, though, my father managed to talk them into it. Among many other traits, good and bad, he was blessed with the gift of salesmanship.

He also placed me with the Catholic welfare agency because he believed that the Catholic foster care system was better than any other option in Los Angeles. One consequence of this, of course, was that I was placed exclusively with Catholic families and sent to Catholic schools.

Between 1942 and 1946, I lived in five foster homes and attended the same number of Catholic schools, bouncing from district to district depending on the location of my new "family." During this period, I even became an altar boy! I could recite "Hail Marys" and "Our Fathers" as well as anyone.

In this light, a letter I wrote my father at the time now strikes me as particularly amusing:

Dear Daddy,

Thank you for the $10.00 you sent me to join the Cub Scouts with. Daddy, do you know anything about my baptismal certificate? I want to make my first Holy Communion. I will be a good Catholic then. . . .

Despite my desire to be a "good Catholic," I continued my disruptive antics. One morning I combed my hair using the holy water in the church sanctuary, but I quickly learned not to do that again. I also enjoyed bringing marbles to school so I could challenge my schoolmates to games and trade marbles with fellow enthusiasts. It didn't take much to get in trouble: giggling, talking out of turn, even chewing gum was an offense—one that I was reprimanded for several times. I can still feel the pain from the nuns' rulers rapping on my knuckles.

FOR FOUR AND A HALF YEARS, I did not see my father at all, though he wrote frequent letters and sent money whenever he could. In his letters, he stressed his love for me and told me how much he missed me. He also dispensed his armchair wisdom, everything from "cleanliness is next to godliness" to "work hard and study," "be a good boy," "eat healthy," and "always dress well." These were the tenets of his life, which I suppose he wanted to pass on to me. As I see it now, his parental neglect was indisputable, though I suppose he felt his letters were one way he could make it up to me.

Whenever I wrote to him about getting into some sort of trouble, he wouldn't hear of it. He would never let me say that I did anything wrong. From his point of view, it was always someone else's fault, the very philosophy he demonstrated in his own life. Even though I tried to take responsibility for my shortcomings and own up to my actions, my father's belief in me actually helped build my self-esteem and allowed me to get through some pretty rough times. And even if I wasn't the perfect kid he believed me to be, I appreciated his unwavering support. In my mind, he was my one and only dad, and he was all I had. Just as he loved me fiercely, I loved him just as much. For all his flaws, his love sustained me. Despite everything, through my young eyes, he appeared to be doing what he could to take care of me—even if it was from afar.

A letter I wrote to my father on July 9, 1945, survived. As I reread it, all my feelings resurface—it's almost as if I wrote it yesterday.

Dear Daddy,

I rec'd your check but I am sorry you didn't write. Daddy, I hope you can come home for my birthday. It seems so long since I saw you. It will be 2 years. It will not [be] like a party if you are not there.

It is very hot out here.

I pass[ed] into the 4th grade.

I am enjoying my vacation. I went to the Coliseum on [the] 4th of July.

I am not an angel. I am not a bad boy. I am just like any child. I am rough and tough. I am no better than any other child, boy, girl, man, woman. Sometimes I start a fight. The boys don't start all the fights. Sometimes it is me.

I love you, Daddy. Your loving son, Eddie

———————

AFTER THE NIGHTMARE of the first foster home, the subsequent homes I landed in were much better, even if some of the parents were fairly aloof. All the homes were middle-class, and I was reasonably comfortable. At one point I even held a job as a newspaper boy at a trolley stop. But I was always the "welfare kid," the hard-luck case, a second-class citizen compared to the other children in the family. I didn't like being looked down upon in that way.

I was an angry child; there's no doubt about that. There was a kind of reverse logic I employed: instead of seeing my father as my deserter, I saw him as my defender. So I felt protective of him, in a way, and resentful of the people who were actually taking care of me! I was aware that my father often had arguments with my foster parents. He would dispute everything from the quality of the care they gave me to their household routines and, most of all, the expenses they claimed. He didn't want to pay them back. Meanwhile, I felt angry on his behalf, as if he were getting a raw deal. I recall telling one of the families that they should be nicer to me because my father was paying them to take care of me. Such a bold statement coming from a young boy's mouth must have infuriated the family. Still, they didn't do anything to try to improve our relationship.

———————————

FROM WINTER TO SPRING OF 1946, I lived briefly with a family by the name of Wellmuth. Mrs. Wellmuth's letter to my father in February of that year paints a fairly accurate portrait of my life as a foster child:

> Dear Lt. Hajim,
>
> I know how worried and concerned you must be about Eddie so I hope this letter reaches you on your return to New York.
>
> I just asked Eddie if he wanted me to tell you anything for him as I was going to write to you. He said, "Just tell him I like it a lot here in fact I love it." He apparently is very happy probably due to the fact that we have a couple of boys for him to play with, we have two, Tommy will be eleven in April and Gerry will be nine in July. It is very nice for all three of them.
>
> Miss Rush from the Catholic welfare told me you wanted Eddie to go to a Catholic school so I have entered him at St. Anselm's, the school our boys go to. It is on the corner of 70th and Van Ness, taught by the Sisters of St. Joseph. He says he likes it very much. He is exceptionally good in arithmetic, he is learning his times tables, he writes them every night for homework.

He is quite interested in Mars, the sun, moon, etc. He is always explaining it to the kids. We get a big kick out of him. . . .

Miss Rush also brought some clothes for him. It was a sad sight when the little fellow opened his suitcase. He just had one pair of pants other than his suit that he could wear to school. His underclothes were rags, except for one new pair of shorts and one undershirt. I had to wash and sew all of his T-shirts and jackets before he could wear them. Miss Rush bought two pairs of pants, two shorts, two undershirts, two white T-shirts, and two colored T-shirts, so he is pretty well outfitted now. . . .

Eddie has been with us three weeks today. Miss Rush told us he would only be here temporar[ily]. We will be glad to keep him here until you are able to make whatever arrangements you think best. We like Eddie very much. He is a fine little fellow. You will be mighty proud of him when you see him. . . .

He said he was supposed to have an allowance. He had $1.76 when he came, of which he still has $1.20. I told him to use that and when it was gone I would give him some and probably by that time you would be home and you would tell us what to do. He is very conservative with his spending. . . .

I hope this letter will help to ease your mind a little and I assure you we will do everything we can to make him as happy as possible.

Sincerely,

Mrs. H. T. Wellmuth

Another letter, dated April 17, 1946, fills in more details:

Dear Mr. Hajim,

I received your check for $60.00 today. Thank you very much. I turned the check over to Miss Rush, as she is back on the job after a month's leave of absence due to the sudden death of her father. . . .

Eddie is fine, and apparently very happy. He has gained six lbs. since he has been with us. He asked me the other day how long he had lived here. When I told him two months the 5th of April, he said, "Gee, I haven't even had one nightmare and I haven't been sick to my stomach, either." Both he and Mrs. Neff told me he has always had nightmares and was usually sick to his stomach a couple of times a month. He was very high-strung and nervous when he came here. He really seems to be getting back down to earth. He has also broken himself of quite a vocabulary of some pretty choice slang words.

I suppose you are wondering why he isn't a Cub yet. He wanted to be in the same Den with Tommy and he had to wait for one of the boys that was moving to get out so he could join as they already had their quota. However, he will be initiated Friday the 26th of April. Mr. Wellmuth took him to the Pack master's house last night to recite his laws, promises, etc. He did very well. He has been visiting the Den meeting the last two weeks.

He is still doing very well in school. Their [report] cards are due again next week after their Easter vacation. I will have him send you his marks. I know you would rather hear from him.

He picked your Easter card out all by himself. I think he did very well, don't you?

Thank you very much for remembering us at Easter. I hope you have a very happy day.

Sincerely,

Mrs. Wellmuth

AFTER THE RATHER PLEASANT EXPERIENCE of living with Mrs. Wellmuth, at long last I was placed with a family who accepted me fully as one of their own. The Robbs had a boy around my age, John. Because Mrs. Robb had been unable to have any more children, she and her husband were open to having a foster child, as they wanted a friend for their son. Fortunately for me, they treated me the same way they treated him, as if there were absolutely no difference between us.

I had never known that kind of love or acceptance. Until then, from my perspective, most of the homes I had lived in had only taken me for the money. And I knew it.

This family—which I quickly came to think of as *my* family—was entirely different. We lived in a big old brown house in Redondo Beach, California. You could cross the Pacific Coast Highway, go down a cliff, and there was the ocean. In fact, we used to play ball right on the Pacific Coast Highway. It was so infrequently traveled in those days that a car would come by only rarely. When it did, we'd move aside, then resume our game as soon as it passed.

I found out later from a newspaper article that John Robb went on to study veterinary medicine at the University of California, Davis. I often think about him and his parents and wish I could thank them for their warmth and attention.

The weeks I spent with the Robbs were some of the happiest of my childhood. It was the first time anyone had truly loved and cared for me. I was never to know that feeling of safety and security again until I became an adult and had a family of my own.

JANAURY 18TH 1946

16—16896

Y DEAR SON EDDIE—
    I WILL LEAVE FOR EUROPE STOPPING IN FRANCE AND
ERMANY FOR ARMY TROOPS TO BRING THEM BACK HOME, THIS ASSIGNMENT WILL
AKE ME AWAY FOR ABOUT 30 DAYS FROM U.S.A. AND RETURNING TO NEW YORK.
HE EXPECTED DEPARTURE DATE IS ABOUT JANAURY 23 OR 24. I AM HAPPY THA
HAVE CONTACTED REV. J.J.TRUXAW OF YOUR FORMER SCHOOL AT 1433 W.9TH
THOUGHT THAT YOU HAD BEEN ATTENDING THAT SCHOOL FOR THE PAST 3 YEAR
RS. NEFF NEVER ADVISED ME OF THE CHANGE, HOWEVER ITS ALL FOR THE BES
LEASE KEEP CLEAN AND HAPPY, I HAVE PAID ALL YOUR BILLS TO MRS. NEFF
ND HAD BEEN PAYING HER FOR YOUR CARE AND BOARD PLUS THE COST OF 1 PA
F SHOES PER MONTH, SO TRY AND BE VERY NEAT, YOUR HAIR, YOUR TEETH, A
NDS ALWAYS BE CLEAN. DONT MIX WITH CHILDREN WHO FIGHT OR ARGUE, I K
OW YOU MISS MY CARE SON, AND HOPE THAT IN THE NEAR FUTURE SAY ABOUT
UR NEXT BIRTHDAY I CAN SEE YOU OR YOU BE WITH ME OR NEAR ME, SONNY
LL CAN NOT HAVE EVERYTHING, I HAVE BEEN THROUGH ALL THE WAR AND WAR
OO AND STILL MAINTAIN EVERTHING AND TRYING TO KEEP YOU HAPPY AND CLE
O, DO YOUR VERY BEST, MRS. NEFF WAS QUITE CARELESS IN CARING FOR YOU
HAD NO WAY OF KNOWING OR TO CONTACT YOU ONLY BY YOUR NICE LETTERS
RITE ME. I HAVE ONLY ONE SINGLE SNAP SHOT PICTURE OF YOU IN THREE
WROTE TO YOU FROM EVERY CORNER OF THE WORLD AND SENT YOU MY PICTURE
OW AND THEN, SO SONNY REMEMBER I LOVE AND YOUR DADDY, THE PICTURES
OOK OF YOU BEFORE THE WAR STAND IN FRONT OF ME DAILY ON MY DESK, YO
OING TO MOVE TO ANOTHER RESIDENTIAL SCHOOL, BETTER THAN YOUR PRESEN
E HAPPY AND WRITE ME.   YOUR DADDY LT. JACK

*One of my dad's
letters to me while
away at sea (1946)*

Age 9 (1945)

CHAPTER THREE

"What Am I Doing Here?"

c: 1946–1950

I N JANUARY OF 1946, I received a mailgram from my father, sent via the US Naval Communication Service and dated the eighteenth of that month. It was the first inkling I had that I might be somehow reunited with my father after the war ended. The concerns my father expressed in the letter were typical of him.

> *My dear son Eddie—*
>
> *I will leave for Europe stopping in France and Germany for army troops to bring them back home. This assignment will take me away for about 30 days from U.S.A. and returning to New York. The expected departure date is about January 23 or 24. I am happy that I have contacted the Rev. J. J. Truxaw of your former school at 1433 W. 9th St. I thought that you had been attending that school for the past 3 years. Mrs. Neff [of the family I had been living with previously] never advised me of the change, however it's all for the best. Please keep clean and happy. I have paid all your bills to Mrs. Neff and had been paying her for your care and board plus the cost of 1 pair of shoes per month. Try and be very neat, your hair, your teeth,*

and hands always be clean. Don't mix with children who fight or argue. I know how you miss my care, son, and hope that in the near future, say about your next birthday, I can see you or you be with me or near me. Sonny, we all cannot have every-thing. I have been through all the war and War 1 too and still maintain everything and trying to keep you happy and clean. So, do your very best. Mrs. Neff was quite careless in caring for you. I had no way of knowing or to contact you only by your nice letters you write me. I have only single snap shot picture of you in three years. I wrote to you from every corner of the world and sent you my picture now and then, so sonny, remember I love [you] and [am] your daddy. The pictures I took of you before the war stand in front of me daily on my desk. You are going to move to another residential school, bet-ter than your present one. Be happy and write me.

Your daddy,

Lt. Jack

I was still living with the Robbs when the mailgram came. Shortly thereafter, Mrs. Robb replied to my father in an undated letter, written in her distinctive backhand, her script angled to the left:

Dear Mr. Hajim,

Edmund was nonplussed by your letter—a little sad, I believe.

However, his daddy is his ideal. The first thing he did on arrival was set up his dresser with your picture.

Our John and he have become great pals. We are very fond of him also, and hope you two have all the happiness in the world together.

We will do everything we can do to prepare him [for] a happy trip in every way.

He has been with us a month but only gained 2 pounds. For some reason we can't fatten him up—he now weighs 66.

You will get a great kick out of him—he is spirited, serious, and ambitious.

School will close Friday June 1st. However, Eddie was promoted to 5th grade upon transfer, so you know he is a good little scholar.

He doesn't care about leaving the old clothes, but he's a marble champ. He started with ten and has twenty-eight pounds (we just weighed them). He won every one—he has to bring those if he has to hold them on his lap. Your pictures and his marbles are his favorite possessions.

I would be especially happy knowing he will be able to make his first holy communion for his birthday. He is all prepared and [I] know how happy you will be with his sincerity. Take good care of him for us and remember should necessity arise and you are not able to have him with you, he will want to be with us—we hope.

Sincerely,

Mrs. Rockwell C. Robb

P.S. We were going to start him with piano lessons next week. Perhaps he will be able to [take them] there. He wants to learn and likes music.

SURE ENOUGH, in mid-1946, my father was discharged from the United States Merchant Marines. He had started out in the Pacific theater but was subsequently transferred to the Atlantic theater, so instead of being discharged in California, he was discharged in New York. There, he was determined to resume his once fruitful life.

After he settled in, he bought me a one-way airline ticket from Los Angeles to New York and somehow persuaded the Catholic welfare agency to let me fly alone to meet him. Though I loved being with the Robbs, I didn't resent leaving them. Enough time had passed so that my feelings of hurt and anger about being left behind by my father had dissipated, and I was eager to see him. In fact, I was really looking forward to our reunion.

In the early summer, I said my goodbyes and boarded the flight with all my worldly possessions, including my prized pet turtle and treasured rock collection. After four stopovers—in Oklahoma City, Denver, St. Louis, and Chicago—I finally arrived. The journey took twenty hours.

After I landed, I was not only tired but also a little sick: I was so nervous before boarding the plane that I ate an entire box of Oreo cookies and became sick on the leg of the trip over the Rockies. That nausea never seemed to go away for the duration of the trip. Still, when I saw my dad at the New York airport, I was genuinely happy to be reunited with him.

To my surprise, however, my father didn't seem particularly glad to see me. For one thing, the plane was very late in arriving. (Those were the days when most flight schedules were unreliable.) And he was a stickler for punctuality. Then he opened my suitcase and discovered that the reason it was so heavy was that I had packed my rock collection in it. To top it all off, he noticed that I didn't have as many clothes as he expected. Where were all the clothes my foster families were supposed to have bought me? he asked. It occurs to me now that maybe he didn't receive Mrs. Robb's letter.

The point is that we hadn't seen each other in *four and a half years*— and this is what he noticed? His anger toward me was very disturbing. At least I had my pet turtle in a little box, which he put in his inside coat pocket on the way from the airport to Manhattan. But I can only imagine that the turtle suffocated during the two-hour taxi ride, because when we arrived at our destination, my father told me it had died. Imagine, the turtle had survived the twenty-hour flight only to succumb to my father's carelessness. I was devastated.

THAT SUMMER, for the first couple of months, the two of us lived in a room at the William Sloane House, a YMCA residence at 356 West 34th Street in Manhattan. But the arrangement wasn't easy for my father. He didn't know what to do with himself or how to go about rebuilding his career. Given that he'd spent the past several years at sea, he wasn't comfortable with the land-based life. He couldn't find steady work, nor could he get along with the relatives of his who were still living in Bensonhurst. He never seemed to enjoy spending time with them—or doing much of anything, for that matter.

By that point, I had grown very independent, especially from my father. Although he never hit me, he was strict, so the new living arrangement was not easy for me, either. Though I never had had any exposure to my father's side of the family, and would have liked it, he seemed to want to keep me away from our Bensonhurst relatives. I had never met any of them. Why? He said he didn't want me around people who spoke a foreign language and had unfamiliar customs! Instead, he wanted me to be as American as possible. As a result, I spent quite a bit of time by myself.

It was around then that I finally mustered the courage to ask my father *how* my mother died. He told me it was while giving birth to a second child. He callously said she didn't like children anyway, and so it was for the best.

His words were so cold, angry, and devoid of emotion. Whenever I asked him about her, I got the same reaction. He never uttered anything positive, kind, or loving when he spoke about her. It finally got to the point where my mother was a verboten subject. So I just stopped asking questions.

It didn't occur to me until many years later that I had never seen a picture of my mother. In later years, my wife, Barbara, often wondered about that. Wasn't it odd for my father not to have kept a photograph of her *somewhere*? If she had actually died, there wouldn't be any reason— certainly not the acrimony of a divorce—to hide her picture from me.

And why didn't I ask him if he had one? I think sometimes children accept what their parents tell them as the truth, even though to outside observers it might seem illogical or far-fetched.

At the end of the summer, we moved to a small one-and-a-half-room apartment on the second floor of the Mermaid Hotel, on Coney Island, so I could enroll in fifth grade at PS 106. Once I got there, I found some refuge in my studies, a safe haven I would come to embrace over the course of my youth. My academic year went well enough, but once again, it was a bad year for my dad, who had grown increasingly despondent over not being able to find a steady job.

In the spring of 1947, however, he applied for and got a position with the merchant marines, this time doing the one thing he knew he was good at—being a radio operator. Unfortunately, it required him to head back to the high seas. This was the only way he could provide for me, and I'm sure he felt he had no choice.

Unsure of how long he'd be gone, he tried finding me a place to stay. A local resident, Mrs. Bernstein, agreed to take me in, to my father's great relief. But at the last minute, just as he was preparing to ship out, Mrs. Bernstein changed her mind and said she couldn't take me until September. That left several weeks in which I would be on my own unless my father was able to find another place—immediately.

For reasons I'm not sure I'll ever understand, my father decided that I would spend the rest of the summer on my own in the hotel! I was eleven years old! He made a deal with a nearby delicatessen so I would always have a place to eat. As he was leaving to report for duty, he gave me some money and told me to stay out of trouble.

For the following few weeks, I lived alone in that hotel room, and it didn't bother me. By that point in my life, I had gotten used to being on my own and had even grown to like it. I took the subway to museums and libraries to escape the hustle and bustle that surrounded me day and night. I went to New York Giants baseball games at the Polo Grounds. I also learned a lot about cards and dice, the games being played on the street in front of the hotel.

Growing up in the late 1930s and '40s—well, I won't say it was a more innocent time in our country or that young people didn't have some of the same sorts of problems as they do now. They certainly did. But it felt different. For the most part, families stayed together and lived in tightly knit communities.

It was also a time when people needed good guys and bad guys. Why?

The good guys gave you someone to believe in. And we stayed loyal to our heroes through thick and thin. Many of my heroes appeared on the big screen—including John Wayne, who starred in *Angel and the Badman* that year, and Gary Cooper, who starred in Cecil B. DeMille's *Unconquered*. I loved going to the movies, and I was greatly influenced by watching westerns and war movies because the cowboys and military heroes always made the best choices and did the right thing. It didn't hurt that John Wayne always seemed to have a tall, voluptuous, darkhaired woman by his side, the picture of perfect womanhood—or at least I thought so at the time.

UNFORTUNATELY, by the beginning of the school year, Mrs. Bernstein decided she could not take care of me after all, so I found myself having to move yet again. From his ship, my father contacted a Jewish welfare agency that found a home for me.

I reported to the Israel Orphan Asylum, at 2540 Beach Channel Drive in Far Rockaway, by myself. It was a group home for boys and girls run by the Jewish welfare agency. Given the name, I wasn't sure if I was being sent to an orphanage or a place where mentally ill people lived. Once I arrived, I was greeted by a woman named Mrs. Hartman. It turns out she was the wife of the head of the institution—Judge Gustave Hartman, for whom a small park on the Lower East Side of Manhattan is named. Mrs. Hartman later wrote a book about her experiences.

I wasn't sure what to expect at my new home, but I knew things were going to be very different. After all, I had suddenly gone from living in my own hotel room, where I had a private bathroom and a place to put my things, to living with fifty other boys in a single communal room. I had to place all my belongings in a drawer under my bed. The bathroom had ten showers and ten toilets in it, and several boys showered together at the same time.

"What am I doing here?" I kept asking myself.

I was introduced to the others as *Eddie—he can read.* This came as a surprise to me because I'd always considered myself a rather slow reader. My grades were okay, but they were nothing to brag about. And I always thought that if my reading skills were better, my grades would have improved. But evidently, I was way ahead of the other students.

One older boy named Rick Safran took me under his wing, warning me on my first day about the usual rites of passage at the orphanage. New boys got pushed around, he said—that was just the way it was. He and I would become very close friends.

Years later, an article that Rick wrote accurately reflected what we were both feeling as boys living in the same home: "We had no choice in the matter. We were orphans. Our parents had somehow disposed of themselves leaving us to get on as best as we could. We became tough and self-sufficient. We didn't cry when we were hurt. Ours was a world punctuated by brawls and struggles in the scramble for adolescent prestige. Love itself was a luxury we could not afford. It had little survival value. Tenderness was something we rarely experienced and certainly never understood. What replaced love was a fierce devotion to one another, to our many championship athletic teams, and to our hazy dreams of capturing a measure of success."

Adjusting to my new surroundings wasn't easy. I thought of living in the orphanage as both a blessing and a curse. In fact, I never felt that I truly belonged because I *had* a father—so in my mind, there was no logical reason for me to be there. Despite my father's rationale for leaving me again, it was hard for me to adjust. I hated being called one of the boys from "the home." I just couldn't understand the reasoning for placing me in the system, which only made me sad and angry. These mounting emotions had no outlet, so I channeled them into my activities, including sports. In retrospect, it seems as if that geyser of feeling gave me a lot of energy and drive, qualities that would later propel me forward in life.

On the other hand, without my realizing it at the time, the orphanage turned out to be an unexpected lucky break for me because I finally found two things I'd never had: *community* and *consistency.* Thankfully, both came at a time in my life when I needed them most, though I had no way of knowing it then.

The orphanage also gave my life a *structure* that it never had before. Life with my father, and life on my own, had been almost freeform; I rarely knew what to expect. In a way, I took comfort in the routines of the institution.

IN THE FALL OF 1947, as I moved from Coney Island and into the orphanage, I left PS 106 and enrolled in PS 104. The school was in a fairly affluent community that was only ten blocks away from the home. It was a fine public school, and I flourished there. I was captain of the crossing guards and even got a medal for my service in that capacity; I was president of my class; I gave the daily "morning report" to the entire school over the PA system; I won a ping-pong contest; and I played basketball.

Still, there were things I missed: I never learned to ride a bicycle, and I couldn't learn to swim because the pool at the home was only three feet deep. Also, I was generally shy and couldn't get over feeling like an outsider, out of place because of my living situation and family background. I was marked as "one of the kids from the home." I wasn't confident about my appearance, either. I was short, only four-foot-six, and weighed just eighty pounds. So my self-image wasn't exactly great. It was an especially tumultuous time because this was the age when I started noticing girls—and girls started noticing me. The girlfriends I had often commented that I was different from the other boys at the home in a *good* way. I was actually surprised that girls would find me interesting at all. The truth is, I guess I *was* different. I was socially awkward and ill at ease. And no matter how hard I tried, I never felt comfortable in my clothes, because nothing fit me properly. I didn't really know how to dress.

Life at the Israel Orphan Asylum was similar to my experience as a student in Catholic school in one way: we had to go to religious services twice a day. There was a temple in the orphanage where services were held, and on Saturdays, we walked to a nearby synagogue, where boys and girls were separated. The food served at the home was kosher. It wasn't Orthodox, but it was close to it.

When I turned thirteen, I had my bar mitzvah along with six or eight other boys in my class. I read the haftorah and took part in every aspect of the ceremony. As a gift for the occasion, the girls in my class bought me a watch, which made me very upset, because I suspected they did it because they felt sorry for me. This is one of the things that made me want to hide my background—I never wanted anyone to give me anything out of pity.

AFTER A TIME, I didn't want to be at the orphanage anymore and spent most of my time trying to figure out where I would go and what I would do next. Sundays were especially difficult, because that's when most of the kids there received visitors.

Not me.

My dad didn't visit very often because he was at sea most of the time. As a result, Sundays and holidays became sad and painful for me. I didn't have anyone coming to see me or anyplace to go. It was tough—perhaps one of the hardest things I've ever dealt with in my life. To this day, Sundays still make me feel melancholy.

True, my father regularly wrote to me, but if he ever thought of returning permanently to New York, he never discussed it. In fact, there was never a lot of dialogue between my father and me about the future. As time went on and I became more independent, we had some bouts of conflict. I became more confident about expressing myself, my behavior fueled by the anger I felt toward him. In some ways, I suppose I was trying to break my bond with him. In addition, for reasons I'm not clear about, after a while he became persona non grata at the orphanage. It was the same pattern all over again—my father complaining about how I was being treated. And of course, it might have had something to do with payments, ones that he was supposed to have made and didn't. During those years, my father would stay in New York whenever he was back in port from one of his trips. If I wanted to see him, I would take the train to Manhattan, which I did many times. He tried his best, even taking me to the Copacabana to celebrate my fourteenth birthday, but he really didn't know what to do with me. I was a teenager, and he had no experience being with children or adolescents. I had essentially raised myself. Throughout my young life, he had been an unreliable parent—here one day, gone the next. He had left me in the care of strangers.

So, yes, our meetings were sometimes happy, but most of the time they were awkward. Sometimes they ended badly, with an argument that created an emotional state I couldn't tolerate. I'd feel incredibly angry or resentful or sometimes even sad and upset when we separated yet again. I started to shield myself from all those emotions: I had to prevent myself from feeling close to him. Or to anyone.

THE FINAL BLOW came in 1950, after one particular trip to Manhattan to visit him. I knocked on his hotel room door, but he wasn't there. I spent most of the day looking for him, but he was nowhere to be found. Just when I thought he couldn't hurt me any more deeply, he did.

I later would refer to this event as my father's "disappearance." It was just one of many. I didn't see or hear from him again for three years! Hard to believe, right?!

After that day in Manhattan, our relationship changed to one of distant but peaceable coexistence. Maybe the nature of our love for each other changed, too. In front of others, I always put the best face possible on my relationship with my father. But I don't think I was very convincing. In fact, some people commented on my father's absence and suggested that maybe our relationship was not as good as I portrayed it to be. I knew the truth but didn't want to see it.

But I never abandoned my love for my father altogether, even though I knew that I was utterly on my own. Still, I held on to the comfort that his love and letters gave me—the sense that I had *someone* in my corner. I remember consoling myself with the thought that he was doing all he could. Besides, what good would it do me to be angry with the only person I had in the world?

JV basketball (1953)

CHAPTER FOUR

"Hajim Legs"—Quick and Determined

c. 1950–1954

BY JUNE OF 1950, I had graduated from PS 104 and enrolled in the ninth grade at Far Rockaway High School.

One of my teachers at PS 104 wrote the following recommendation for me as I made the transition:

> *To Whom It May Concern:*
>
> *Edmund Hajim of PS 104–Queens is a real leader, selected by the pupils as captain of the school guards and class president. He is an outstanding athlete and student. All his marks are excellent, and the teachers rate his personality as the highest in our school.*
>
> *Henry A. Charlton*

The letter made me proud, but it still didn't take away the pain of my father's disappearance. I didn't think anything would ever erase that pain entirely.

Decades later, in 2014, I discovered the reason for his absence: when a librarian at the University of Rochester was going through former New York governor Thomas E. Dewey's papers, which had been donated to the university, she found among them several documents relating to a legal case my father had instigated. It seems he had been fired from his job as a radio operator—or at least fired from the union to which he belonged—and in response my father sued. In his suit, he claimed that several of the men on board his ship had tried to kill him. He apparently appealed to the governor's office—for help.

I wondered why the matter of a lawsuit would be enough to cause my father to disappear, to stop all contact with me. He'd been in dire straits before, but he hadn't completely vanished from my life in those cases. Maybe during the trial, the judge had forbidden him to travel. Maybe he really did fear for his safety; maybe he had no money and felt ashamed. I don't think I'll ever know the answers. It was painful for me to read about this incident in the governor's papers, and I'm still not sure how much more I want to know about it.

―――――――――

MY FRESHMAN YEAR at Far Rockaway proceeded uneventfully. But when I was in the middle of my sophomore year, in the fall of 1951, I was told that I had to move out of the Israel Orphan Asylum because I was too old to be living there. I was then fifteen, and as a result of my father's disappearance, I had become a ward of the state. I was told that my father was no longer responsible for me, and that if he were ever to come to the orphanage, he would not be welcome. I surmise now that this might have been because he owed them money.

By law, the state had the right to send me anyplace it wanted to, and I was worried that I might end up in a home for "wayward boys" or in a reform school. Thankfully, someone within the system took a look at my academic record—I maintained a high average—and recognized that I had excellent academic potential. The decision was therefore made to place me in the Hebrew National Orphan Home in Yonkers, New York, which would allow me to attend Theodore Roosevelt High School.

I arrived at the HNOH with some trepidation. To my relief, there were only three boys to a room, a far more comfortable arrangement than existed at the Israel Orphan Asylum. There was even a photography lab and a woodshop in the basement. But unlike the IOA, the HNOH was an all-boys residence. Also unlike the IOA, it had a basketball court, where I spent many hours honing my skills, trying to develop a competitive edge, and working off some of my emotional energy.

When I arrived, I was surprised—and delighted—to find my old buddy Rick Safran from the IOA. It was nice to see a familiar face.

The headmaster at HNOH, Reuben Koftoff (nicknamed the Boss), was a wonderful man who took a great interest in all the boys. Although he was very kind to me, I wasn't good at taking direction from him or from anyone else. He did his best to show me that he wanted me to do well. He even tried to mentor me, but at the time I didn't know how to accept help.

Being as stubborn as I was, I didn't think I actually needed help. In my mind, I didn't belong there in the first place. And besides, I was content to "do my own thing" with no paternal direction. I came to like being an outsider looking in. I thought that made me strong and independent.

In retrospect, I was wrong.

The transition was tough. As Rick had once said of IOA, there were definite rites of passage at HNOH, too, that required showing you would fight back when provoked, even if you ultimately lost the battle. But eventually I found my place in the group. I understood the chance I had been given to be at an institution like this, so I took my lumps and carried on. I did everything I could to adjust to my new surroundings.

Most of us learn to make moral decisions early in life, because we have our parents to set an example for us. But having bounced around as much as I did, I had to set my moral compass by taking the measure of the various situations I found myself in.

Eleanor Roosevelt once said, "It's not fair to ask of others what you are not willing to do yourself." My moral exemplars were the people who sacrificed their own comfort for the sake of the greater good, who were generous with their time and offered guidance and a steadying hand. People like Reuben Koftoff, whom everyone revered; Mrs. Benson, my first surrogate parent; and Mrs. Robb, who didn't have to treat me well, but did. They clearly weren't in it for the money. They were there to help and care for needy children.

These people had what I call heart. They had empathy. They took a genuine interest in me in ways I couldn't or simply didn't recognize at the time. But later, I would come to appreciate their indelible influence on me. They inspired me to implement their compassionate and caring ways in my own dealings with people, especially in my business life.

AS FATE WOULD HAVE IT, attending Roosevelt High School provided me with yet another lucky break. It was an excellent school, and it gave me the opportunity to break out of my circumstances and discover my strengths. My fellow students were motivated and showed lots of initiative. In fact, my time at Roosevelt overlapped with a person who would go on to make a name for himself in the world of journalism—Pulitzer Prize winner and Harvard alumnus David Halberstam (1934–2007), who graduated with the class of 1951.

At Roosevelt, I concentrated on getting good grades and excelling at sports. I decided that success in high school was my only hope of achieving a scholarship to college, since I knew my father could not help me financially. To me, college represented freedom from the life I was living—the ability to do whatever I wanted and the flexibility to chart the course of my own life. Being able to make my own decisions and achieving financial independence became my most important goals.

I also decided to channel my energy into sports, fiercely determined to become a good athlete and prove to my high school buddies that I was more than just "that boy from the home." Unlike many people my size, I played basketball; even though I was still relatively short—despite having grown five inches during my sophomore and junior years—I was quick and determined. I also played baseball on the varsity team for two years. I ended up lettering in both sports. In my senior year, the basketball team won the county championship, and the baseball team beat the best team in the league, which resulted in the newspaper headline:

HAJIM LEGS AND MAMARONECK ERRORS RESULT IN ROOSEVELT WIN

That day I had a couple of crucial hits and stole three bases, including home.

In addition to my athletic and academic accomplishments, I managed to make a number of friends in both the home and in the neighborhood—including a few girlfriends. Despite the odds against me, I actually thrived in high school.

As I approached my graduation date, I thought I had at last found a way to take direct control of the path before me—and that way was through college. And I set the goal even higher, because I wanted to go to a private college away from New York City. Most boys from the home—if they went to college at all—would go to local public colleges. I knew a college education would open doors for me, though I still needed to figure out how I was going to pay for it. At the time, it certainly presented a huge challenge for an orphan with no financial resources or any other kind of support system.

I had always held jobs when I was in high school; it was part of my plan for ensuring a secure future of self-determination. My jobs included being a bagger in a grocery store, a pinsetter in a bowling alley, and a soda jerk in a candy store. During the summer after my senior year, I also worked at Camp Delawaxen, in Lackawaxen, Pennsylvania, where I managed the camp's retail store. That experience provided me with an early, if minor, exposure to business success: I learned how to get rid of inventory before the season ended by lowering prices and promoting the remaining goods. By the time I graduated, I had saved $200, a substantial sum in the early 1950s but obviously not enough to pay for college tuition.

THROUGHOUT HIGH SCHOOL, my interests skewed heavily toward math and science, especially chemistry. As time went on, I turned my passion for these subjects into a love of engineering. I reasoned that chemicals were at what was then the forefront of technological innovation, and engineers had a better chance of getting a job than those in other fields.

I couldn't wait to get a new textbook so I could learn more. I even loved the way a new book smelled. When the time came to apply to colleges, I decided that chemical engineering was the career path I was going to pursue, even though I really did not know what chemical engineers did.

In those days, Roosevelt High School allowed its students to apply to a maximum of three colleges. Fortunately, I learned about a New York State scholarship that would pay a good portion of my tuition if I qualified. I applied to three schools in New York—Cornell University, Rensselaer Polytechnic Institute, and the University of Rochester—and was accepted by all three! I had done well in school, yes, graduating fourteenth out of approximately four hundred students. Even so, I didn't get the New York State scholarship. This was quite a blow to me. And yet I still didn't give up hope.

The universe often delivers what we need exactly when we need it. You see, while I was trying to figure out how to pay for college, I had also applied for and was awarded a Naval Reserve Officers Training Corps scholarship. I can still see the award letter: it started out by saying that I was not selected as an awardee, but it went on to say—in the final paragraph—that I was selected as an alternate and was high enough on the list to expect to receive the scholarship. I reread the letter at least a dozen times and stopped in a church that was close by to say a prayer of thanks.

In addition, Reuben Koftoff from HNOH arranged for me to receive a small scholarship from some of the orphanage funds under his control. I've never forgotten that gesture or his support of my education. Most important, I've always remembered that he believed in me. Knowing I could pursue my studies beyond high school without undue financial stress was nothing short of a dream come true.

These rays of light and hope stood in stark contrast to the fact that my father didn't come to my high school graduation. Given his record as a father, I guess I should not have been too surprised. By that time, he had returned from his disappearance and resumed sending me the occasional letter and making sporadic visits. Yet he somehow couldn't make the effort to see me graduate. I had no family at my graduation at all. A whole cauldron of feelings about this disappointment was bubbling inside me, including anger, shame, and confusion. Compared to my classmates, with their families all around them, I felt more alone than ever. But in the end, I chose to put a lid on that cauldron and keep it tightly closed. I had become quite accomplished at suppressing what I was feeling in order to keep functioning as well as I could.

THE NROTC SCHOLARSHIP allowed me to enroll at any one of fifty-two colleges. I chose the University of Rochester because it was the only one of the three New York schools I'd been accepted to that would allow me to graduate in four years. I'd wind up with an engineering degree *and* with my NROTC requirements complete. Both Cornell and RPI indicated that it would take five years, and I didn't think I would be able to afford the fifth year. Cornell also required chemical engineers to study German, and languages were one of my weak suits.

Attending the University of Rochester was the first shot I had at beginning anew, my chance to wipe the slate clean and make a fresh start. I had become extremely determined to create a good life for myself against all odds. I never wanted to look in the rearview mirror and see the road behind me. I only wanted to look ahead. For me, Rochester was the only way to obtain everything I never had as a child—a loving, devoted family; financial security, which would mean that I never needed to worry about money again; and a bright future full of possibilities, over which I would have complete control. At least that's what I hoped for.

Wearing my famous black leather jacket (1953)

CHAPTER FIVE

Driven to Succeed

c. 1954–1958

I ARRIVED AT THE UNIVERSITY OF ROCHESTER CAMPUS in the fall of 1954 alone with just a black leather jacket and an ROTC scholarship.

Let me explain. First, my clothes were cheap-looking and way out of style. I stuck out like a sore thumb among my fellow students. My black leather jacket didn't fit in with the more conservative clothes other people were wearing. And no one I saw on campus had my kind of haircut, so my appearance contributed to my feeling of self-consciousness.

In addition, inwardly, I chose to lock up my past and bury it for good. I vowed never to speak of my origins. I didn't want my classmates to know where I came from or how hard I had to work to get there. If someone asked about my past, I didn't answer. I felt so ashamed of it all—the orphanages, the poverty, the loss of my mother and abandonment by my father, the years of feeling so lonely and isolated. In my mind, keeping my past secret was the only way I could break free from it. It was as if I had to cut off the reality of my past to build a new future.

I think the new friends I met sensed my secrecy and sensitivity. Once they saw how I reacted to their inquiries, they quickly backed off and knew not to "go there" with me. There was one classmate from high school who also was attending Rochester, but I made it clear to him that I didn't want my past discussed.

Because my father was part of that past, I placed all the letters Dad had written to me in boxes and stored them away. I told everyone he was a merchant marine and spent most of his time at sea. If I was asked, I'd say that my mom died in childbirth, because that's what my father had told me. I made no further information available. The truth was, I was humiliated and embarrassed by my past—and that included my father, a man who despite his talents was never able to support me emotionally or financially.

Expending all this energy covering up gave me a dark side. I often felt a return of the rage I had experienced during my childhood. But as I look back on it now, I can see that this inner turmoil also drove me to succeed in ways I could never have imagined. Back in those days, going to therapy was uncommon, so I didn't seek professional help in dealing with my feelings, even though I needed it. Instead, I just continued to keep myself as busy as possible, piling extracurricular activities on top of the very rigorous academic program I'd chosen for myself.

———————

AFTER PLAYING FRESHMAN BASKETBALL AND BASEBALL, I chose not to try out for the varsity teams. Academics and extracurricular activities became more important to me, and I knew I didn't have much of a future as a professional athlete. I played three years of intramural football, basketball, and baseball. Intramural sports gave me the opportunity to enjoy the camaraderie of being part of a team and the rush of adrenaline I got from competition—without the practice requirements of the varsity teams.

During my freshman year, I served on the integration committee, which was responsible for combining the women's campus, called the Prince Street Campus, with the men's campus, called the River

Campus. At the time, the two campuses sat five miles apart. Even though the university had been admitting women since 1900, men moved to the River Campus upon its completion in 1930, and the women had been separate ever since. The integration was successfully completed in 1955. As a freshman I was rejected by all the fraternities—probably because of my appearance and because all but one fraternity didn't take Jewish students. I didn't think of my appearance as a big deal, but I guess it was. As my freshman year progressed, I cut my hair in a crew cut, bought some new clothes, and was helped by a residence-hall mate, Ed Kaplan, who lent me a few of his suits. Fortunately, he was exactly my size, and his father was a haberdasher. Another hall mate, a sophomore named Zane Burday, befriended me early on and counseled me on what to do and not do. His organic chemistry notebook was instrumental in getting me and a number of others through the course. He graduated Phi Beta Kappa, became a doctor, and was my internist for thirty years. He died a few years ago and, as I said at his funeral, he did so much for so many but never asked for anything for himself.

In my sophomore year, my new look and campus activities resulted in my being pledged by Theta Chi fraternity, making me the first Jewish pledge in the one hundred years of the organization's history. My fraternity brothers were a great group of guys, and pledging was a real milestone for me. In my junior year, I became the social chairman, my job being to take charge of the events the fraternity held each Saturday night. During my tenure, I dreamed up a party for the month of February called the Beachcombers Ball. In all modesty, it turned out to be one of the fraternity's best parties ever, and it became a tradition for a number of years.

I really enjoyed participating in projects that took me in various directions that I wouldn't otherwise have explored. I was in all three honor societies; I was chairman of the university's finance board, which distributed money for campus activities; I was one of fifteen elected student government representatives; I was chairman of the engineering council; I was business manager of the dramatic society, responsible for filling the theater for every show; and I was a member of the yearbook staff. I was Mr. Involved!

———————

IN ADDITION TO EVERYTHING ELSE, in my sophomore year I got the idea to start a humor magazine modeled along the lines of *The Harvard Lampoon*. It was called *UGH* (for *UnderGraduate Humor*), and it didn't come into being until my junior year. Although I was seen by most people as a pretty serious guy, I also had, and continue to have, a very dry sense of humor. (As Barbara says, I'm not always fun, but I *am* funny.)

At the time, I thought the students could use an infusion of levity, especially my fellow engineers, who spent more time studying and working in the lab than anything else. The engineering program was tough on all of us, and a large number of students flunked out each year. In my junior year, when the magazine was launched, I was taking organic and physical chemistry plus a couple of other demanding courses. I had six eight o'clock classes and a laboratory every afternoon.

To get the magazine started, I first put together a blue-ribbon group of students to help get the project approved by the president and deans, who were not really in favor of what they considered to be a frivolous project. The administrators were a little touchy at first because they weren't sure what to expect. Was the magazine going to be farcical? Satirical? Would it mock "the system"? I gave the university every assurance that my goal was to entertain the reader and not embarrass the school, and the officials eventually gave us the green light.

Then the staffers and I went out and collected all the various humor magazines we could find from around the country. We studied the best features from each and adapted them to produce a prototype of the first issue.

As it turned out, I really liked entrepreneurialism—especially sales—and I still do.

To finance the publication of the first issue, we went to local merchants, knocking on the doors of every kind of establishment, from bars and hamburger joints to hardware stores and gas stations, all in an effort to sell them ad space. It was a risky buy for them because it was a new magazine with no track record to point to. We were selling enthusiasm—and passion. I learned a very important lesson that year: if you can sell something that does not yet exist to people you have never met before, you will have a leg up on life.

Luckily for us, there was obviously latent demand for humor on campus, since we sold out the first print run in forty-five minutes. I got a big kick out of the fact that the librarian, who was originally not in favor of the project, later came begging for a few copies to put into the archives. Fortunately, I was able to save a few copies for myself and have held on to them to this day. Once you launch a start-up like that, nothing else seems terribly hard. I discovered that when you operate on passion, it isn't work. It's pleasure.

BECAUSE I HAD NOWHERE TO GO during most summers and holidays, and because I needed the money, I worked multiple jobs during those periods. My scholarship only gave me fifty dollars a month, so money was always tight. Working was a necessary means of survival. My jobs ranged from waiting tables to working in the college laundry, to removing railroad ties from an abandoned rail line. When I needed a typewriter in order to write my papers, I wrote to a manufacturer and offered to sell its products on campus if it would give me one as a sample that I could also use for my own needs. The manufacturer took me up on it, even though I only wound up selling one typewriter in two years. I also worked at a local foundry, the post office, and on a Saint Lawrence Seaway construction site. In my senior year, to earn extra income, I became a resident adviser in the dorms.

At one job I had during the summer between my junior and senior years, I waited tables at a Bob's Big Boy restaurant from 6:00 p.m. until 1:00 a.m. When I got off work, I would sleep for a few hours, then head over to the university library, where I helped with various tasks during the day. It was a perfect job because when I wasn't busy, I could doze off. One morning, however, the librarian caught me sleeping.

"Shhh. Don't wake him. He works nights," I heard her whisper to her colleague.

I will always remember what a kind lady she was.

Working all these jobs gave me the opportunity to test several career paths and meet all kinds of people. I discovered that we all have our own joys, our own passions—enthusiasms that inspire us to get out of bed every morning. Even more important, I understood that we can react the opposite way, too, in response to our own aversions. There's great benefit in trying new experiences, especially when you're young. Each job, each experience you have, moves you closer to your calling. And there's no better time than college to experiment, to try new things, so you can become the person you were meant to be.

I had another life-altering epiphany that year. I realized that the more involved I got in extracurricular activities and the more groups I joined, the more my passion for science and math began to shift and turn into a keen interest in *managing* people. I felt as though this was truly my calling.

I loved putting projects and people together to solve a problem.

Even greater was my desire to help people do better than they believed they could do, just as I had been helped in the past by teachers and foster parents.

The University of Rochester has a motto, *Meliora*, which translates into "ever better."

I don't know if that motto rubbed off on me, but ever since I realized my calling, that philosophy has been something I have strived to inspire in others. It has carried into everything I've done. My unwavering drive for improvement motivated me to strive to be a little bit better than I was and then encourage others to do the same.

When you can lead people—whether it's a group of twenty or a group of two thousand—to believe they are better than they think they are, they feel good about themselves and become more productive. That's really what life is all about. If you can do that, ultimately you will have a success story to tell.

———————

ON A COUPLE OF CHRISTMAS HOLIDAYS, I was invited to my classmates' homes and gratefully accepted the invitations. My friends Dick Wedemeyer and Al "Jesse" James (yes, that's his real name; he was my sophomore roommate) were particularly kind. But seeing them interact with their families was emotionally difficult for me. There they were, in the midst of a happy reunion, being so affectionate and having so much fun, which caused me to reflect on the lack of familial warmth in my own life.

Several months after launching the first issue of *UGH*, I went on a visit to the home of my good friend David Melnick—a year younger than I—who was going to be the next editor of the magazine. Of course, I wanted to pass on to him all the information he would need to take over the magazine, but I also enjoyed his company and wanted to spend time with him. While I was there, I met his younger sister, Barbara, for the first time. She was a pigtailed thirteen-year-old—seven years younger than I. To me, she was my friend's kid sister. Cute, of course, but the thought never crossed my mind that we might someday become a couple.

Later I would learn that Barbara had a teenage crush on me from that very first meeting. She thought I was cute, too. And funny. But we wouldn't see each other again until seven years later!

At the time of my first visit with the Melnicks, I was concentrating on more immediate concerns. I had a growing realization that by the end of my junior year, there would no longer be an enormous gap between where I was and where I wanted to go in life. In fact, I felt as though the brass ring was within my grasp. I could visualize my goal because I knew what I wanted. The mosaic of who I was had begun to take shape.

What I didn't know at the time was how important it was to find the right life partner.

Sure, I had thought about getting married. I wanted the beautiful movie-star wife I saw on the big screen. I also wanted a white picket fence, a house in the suburbs, the whole package. In short, I wanted the life I never had, giving my children the love that I was denied. I wasn't going to settle or compromise my principles until I could turn that vision into reality. But there were things I had to do first. I had to leave behind my college relationships because I just wasn't ready. That dream would have to wait.

Aboard the USS Okanogan *with the Command Effectiveness award for engineering, E (January 1960)*

CHAPTER SIX

The Ensign and the Engineer

c. 1958–1962

I GRADUATED FROM THE UNIVERSITY OF ROCHESTER in 1958 with a degree in engineering—and a B minus average. That might sound like nothing to brag about. But let me tell you: the University of Rochester really beat up on engineers. We had to take organic chemistry with the premed students and physical chemistry with the physicists.

I started out third in my class of sixty; by the time I graduated, I was third in my class of six. Only two people in our class made Tau Beta Pi, the engineering honor society, and I wasn't one of them. I was just lucky to graduate in four years—twelve or thirteen of my classmates didn't manage to do that. They eventually did graduate, but it took them a year or two longer.

After graduation, I was required to spend three years on active duty in the navy as an officer. I soon learned that I'd be training for six weeks at Naval Amphibious Base Coronado, near San Diego. Then I would report to the USS *Okanogan* (APA-220[1]), a personnel carrier—picture all

---

[1] APA stands for "auxiliary personnel, attack," a term coined by the navy in 1942. It means that the ship was designed not only to carry troops, but also to carry out assault operations. The number 220 was the number stenciled on its hull.

those transport ships with rope ladders hanging over the sides—that was stationed in the Far East. I would be training to be an engineering officer. Initially, this looked like a pretty dull assignment, but it turned out to be great experience.

To get from Rochester to California, a fraternity brother and I drove to San Diego using a car that belonged to one of our NROTC instructors, Lieutenant Nix. Because the lieutenant didn't have time to drive across the country to see his family in San Diego, he would fly back later on, happy that we would deliver his car. You can imagine: two twenty-two-year-olds, fresh out of college, in a white Cadillac convertible. Let's just say it was a memorable trip!

The first six weeks of basic training required learning everything from shipboard damage control and naval engineering to aerial bombardment and operating landing boats, or LCVPs,[2] which delivered marines to combat beaches. Besides the intensive studying and vigorous physical training, we did spend a certain number of hours in the local bars and hangouts. I was single, after all!

The next step was to meet my ship, which was supposed to be docked in Yokosuka, Japan. When I arrived, I learned it was on a mission, the location of which was classified at a level above what was permissible for anyone in our transportation department to know, so I was free to do what I wanted while I waited for it to return.

I picked up enough Japanese to travel throughout the country for around five weeks and enjoy the sights. But when I ran low on money and couldn't afford to go on any more tourist adventures, I had to find out where the ship was located so I could report for duty. I finally bought the local naval intelligence officer a number of drinks and told him my problem. After he let me know where the ship was, the transportation department flew me to Okinawa, where the *Okanogan* had come into port.

When I reported aboard, I was immediately appointed the A division officer, responsible for all the ship's engines and repair work. At

---

[2] LCVP stands for "landing craft, vehicle, personnel"; it's also known as a Higgins boat.

the age of twenty-two I was in charge of 180 men, ranging in age from eighteen to nearly fifty. It was more responsibility than I would have for many years to come. The men under my command included two warrant officers, the carpenter (Chips), and the electrician (Sparks), both of whom were old enough to be my father and, fortunately, took me under their wings. That first year was a true learning experience like no other. I knew every engine on the ship and every pipe in the engine room—how they operated and what happened if they malfunctioned. I also understood what the ship could and could not do.

Our ship was used for all kinds of special duty. Over the course of three years, we made seven crossings of the Pacific. The *Okanogan* was at one point a hotel ship in Hong Kong—a headquarters ship that serves as the naval authority in port. It takes responsibility for shore patrol, and can act as a temporary residence if needed. At another point, it carried fifty-two tons of purchases made by navy wives from Hong Kong to Subic Bay, in the Philippines. It also acted as a festival ship in Beppu, allowing local residents to visit. On another mission, it transported a shipment of golden Buddhas from Thailand to Los Angeles. Each of the Buddhas was ten to fifteen feet tall.

During my last year, we got stuck for nearly five months in San Francisco while the ship was in the shipyard. That was okay with me: I not only fell in love with the city, I also fell in love with a local young lady. Her parents loved me, too, but nixed the deal because I wasn't Catholic.

Thankfully, the closest I got to combat in Vietnam was when the *Okanogan* put some of its boats up the Mekong River with SEALs and Delta Force personnel on board. This was before the war broke out in full force.

THE NAVY OFFERED a wide range of experiences and choices that would test any man's principles and mettle. I could go out at night, drink beer, chase women, and/or spend every evening watching a movie in the officers' mess. All these activities were expected—they were the norm, and of course I wanted to fit in. But I also knew I was relatively uneducated when it came to the liberal arts, so I used some of my time to read the so-called great books, including epic tomes like *Beowulf* and the *Iliad*. My only previous instruction in the liberal arts had come from taking two semesters of English literature and one semester of economics in college.

During my last two years in the navy, in an effort to test my interest in business, I took courses in accounting and business law through the extension arm of the University of California, Berkeley. I thought I might be interested in law, and I even became a prosecutor on board the ship for a military court called Rocks and Shoals, which was held at sea. I also practiced being a defense attorney. Though I enjoyed being a defender, I really didn't love either aspect of being a lawyer. However, I was grateful for the opportunity to try my hand at it because it gave me a chance to realize that practicing law wasn't for me.

The navy also offered me a virtual treasure trove full of stories—I've been dining out on them for years. I often regale my companions with some of my favorites, including the one about the quartermaster whose stepfather was younger than he was; then there's the one about the young seaman who had just gotten married and wanted to see the captain but wouldn't tell me why. (It turns out that he wanted to ask the captain how to make babies and thought I was too young to know the answer.) Then there's the one about the pilot who approached Bangkok harbor at breakneck speed, a dangerous maneuver over which the captain and I disagreed. The captain was angry with me until after we docked and the pilot told him that he was putting the journey "in Buddha's hands." If something were to happen, the pilot said, it was meant to be.

By the end of my time in the navy, in 1961, I had served under four captains, Amos T. Hathaway being the most famous and the most difficult. (But that's another story.) The ship was awarded a green E—the *E* is the navy's shorthand for Command Effectiveness Awards—for excellence in damage control and a red E for excellence in engineering.

In my last year, I qualified as special sea detail officer of the deck. This position allowed me to oversee the pilots who took the ship in and out of major ports. I was also a command duty officer, which allowed me to act on behalf of the captain if he happened not to be on board. These are two accomplishments I am extremely proud of to this day.

Most important, the navy gave me three precious gifts: first, it trained me to become *deliberate* in everything I do. Second, it showed me that every mission needs *well-defined rules*, followed to the letter, in order to ensure success. And third, it showed me that no mission can be accomplished without a *well-motivated team* on board.

I had given the navy my all, and my superiors wanted me to sign up for another three years of duty. But the only way I was going to do that was if they gave me my own ship. Ultimately, I wanted my own command and thought I had what it took; I'd certainly met all the necessary requirements to become a captain.

Although I knew that my ambition might have seemed unrealistic to some, the navy did sometimes assign young officers to the command of forty-foot minesweepers and other small vessels. For a while it looked like it might actually happen. But I was told I had to serve as an executive officer first. This was not an option, because I had heard horror stories from friends who had taken that route.

By the end of my three years, I had accomplished almost everything I set out to do. I qualified for every duty; I received awards and accolades from my commanding officers; I had taken business courses and had actually applied and was accepted to business school at UC Berkeley. In my heart and gut, I knew it was the right time to move on.

DURING MY TIME IN THE NAVY, my father moved peripherally in and out of my life. His disappearance in 1950 had taken its toll, but we continued to correspond and see each other occasionally. By this time, he had taken up with an older woman named Lillian, who had a penthouse apartment in San Francisco. I visited them a number of times. It was his only significant relationship with a woman—that I know of—since his divorce from my mother.

My relationship with Dad had become perfunctory—not terribly warm. I thought it was nice that he had someone in his life. He was still quite difficult to be with, but Lillian and I got along very well. In fact, having her there during our visits made them a lot more pleasant. However, near the end of my military service, Dad and I had a pretty bad falling-out after I told him I was leaving the US Navy. He became very upset with me for giving up "a secure career in the service."

Deciding to leave the navy seemed like a perfectly logical next step to me, but my father vigorously objected to it, and it further distanced us. I felt he really didn't understand me and was basing his feelings on his own experiences—which had led to a definite sense of insecurity about money. He couldn't see me taking a risk to better myself, giving one thing up to find an even better one. Also, I believe the highlight of his life was being a commissioned officer in the merchant marines. He couldn't imagine me giving up my position. In the end, I think he wanted me to be safe, and he didn't want me to repeat his mistakes.

BEFORE I WAS DISCHARGED, I applied for engineering jobs in and around San Francisco, but there was nothing in my field. (If there had been, perhaps I might have gotten in on the early stages of Silicon Valley.)

In the absence of an offer in the Bay Area, I sent out forty-plus résumés across the country, which produced two job offers back East: one in Lexington, Kentucky, with DuPont, and the other in Wilmington, Delaware, with the Hercules Powder Company. The latter opening was for an applications research engineer in plastics. You may remember that 1967 was the year of *The Graduate*, the film in which Dustin Hoffman's character, fresh out of college, was told by an older, well-meaning party guest, "I just want to say one word to you, just one word . . . *plastics*. There's a great future in plastics. Think about it." Well, even though the movie wouldn't come out for another six years, I had the same feeling about plastics, so I accepted the job in Wilmington.

At the time, Hercules was in the midst of developing polypropylene, the market for which it would later dominate. Besides, Wilmington was much closer than Lexington was to Philadelphia, Washington, DC, and New York—cities I thought of as "civilization."

Just before leaving the navy, I bought a light blue 1957 VW bug for $600 and used it to drive east, arriving in Wilmington in July. My job was to support around twenty salesmen who were pioneering the sale of two new products, Hyfax (polyethylene) and Pro-fax (polypropylene.)

Each morning there were a number of requests to test this or that or make a certain material stronger, lighter, or shinier. I wore a white coat, had an assistant, and worked in a laboratory all day churning out answers. I felt as though I were really making a difference, because every day presented a challenge that I met by constructing experiments that would find solutions.

After being at Hercules for a short time, I got to know several engineers who had been on the job for twenty years or more. It became clear to me that I didn't want to follow that path. They were part of the corporate bureaucracy, somewhat bored and living on fixed salaries, having seemingly hit a ceiling. I knew I wanted a position in which the sky was the limit. In addition, they seemed vulnerable to changes in technology and company strategy, with no job security. For example, one entire group working on water chemicals was let go when the company decided to abandon its efforts in that area.

Someone at Hercules pointed out that the best course of action for me was to go back to school and study business so I could combine it with my engineering degree. That seemed like a viable idea, although I originally thought you didn't have to go to college to learn about business. Still, I realized that maybe my colleague was right: the chemicals industry was interesting, but, contrary to what Dustin Hoffman's character was told in *The Graduate*, perhaps its future was not so bright.

While I worked full-time at Hercules during the day, at night I started taking classes at the Wharton School, which was affiliated with the University of Pennsylvania. Three nights a week, I'd get in my Volkswagen and drive the forty-five minutes to Philadelphia to attend class; then I'd drive the forty-five minutes back to Delaware. I have to admit that many nights I stopped at watering holes on the way that were patronized by the young and the beautiful—people who were supposedly attending ski club meetings or other "legitimate" functions. Right!

One of my professors at Wharton told me he thought I was wasting my time in the night school program. He thought I should go to business school full-time. "You're not like the other people here," he said. "You're studying with people who are just trying to get through. Go someplace where you will be challenged."

This professor had a point.

I had been working at Hercules for about a year when my boss gave me a 5 percent raise, which equaled around thirty extra dollars a month. Since I believed that I had done a great job, I didn't understand the low percentage. When I questioned my boss about the raise, his response was, "You're young, you're a bachelor, and you don't need more money."

That felt so wrong.

A few months earlier, I had traveled to Boston to see some friends. While I was there, I visited my Rochester classmate (and fellow chemical engineer and naval officer) Dick Wedemeyer, who was attending Harvard Business School. He was adamant that I apply to Harvard as soon as possible.

At first, I thought I could never get in. But then I began to reconsider. My boss's weak defense of my low raise, combined with my Wharton professor's strong assessment of my skills, left me determined to make yet another change.

I walked around the Harvard campus thinking, "Someday I am going to be here." I kept a positive attitude: not only could I get here, but I could also be successful here. I was willing to step out of my comfort zone to pursue my passion.

I filled out an application, even though it was a little late in the year to be doing so. Thankfully, one of my commanding officers in the navy wrote a very strong letter of recommendation for me and, through the grace of God, I got in.

There was just one problem. I didn't have the money to pay the tuition. Or did I?

I had $5,000 in savings, which was all the money I had to my name. Coincidentally, it was just enough to pay the first year's tuition. I didn't know how I was going to pay for the second year, much less cover my other expenses. But it didn't matter. I had to take this chance and turn it into my next opportunity. And I'm glad I did, because Harvard Business School changed my life.

HARVARD UNIVERSITY

AT CAMBRIDGE IN THE COMMONWEALTH OF MASSACHUSETTS

THE PRESIDENT AND FELLOWS OF HARVARD COLLEGE, acting on the recommendation of the Faculty of Business Administration and with the consent of the Honorable and Reverend the Board of Overseers, have conferred on

EDMUND A HAJIM

the degree of Master in Business Administration with distinction.

In witness whereof, by authority duly committed to us, we have hereunder placed our names and the University seal on this eleventh day of June in the Year of Our Lord nineteen hundred and sixty-four and of Harvard College the three hundred and twenty-eighth.

MBA diploma from the Harvard Business School

Section F of the Harvard Business School class of 1964

CHAPTER SEVEN

Business Boot Camp—and Eagles and Gophers

c. 1962–1964

IARRIVED AT HARVARD IN THE FALL OF 1962. Before I could park my Volkswagen, one of my can mates (eight of us shared a bathroom) had already gone over to the dean's office about having a foreign student living with him. Even my roommate Roger wanted a veteran from New England and got the veteran, but his home address was a post office box in San Francisco.

The admissions office told him, "Mr. Hajim is a naval officer born in Los Angeles." That reply seemed enough for Roger to consent to having me as a roommate. But on our way to our first breakfast together, as I was chattering on, which I tend to do, he said, "I don't talk in the morning." I took the hint.

In spite of that rocky start, Roger and I became very good friends and remain so to this day. Roger was a naval aviator who attended Yale and was from a fine old New England family. I even introduced him to his wife via his wife's brother, who sat next to me in class. (Sadly, I attended his wife's funeral in 2019. She and Roger were married for fifty-five years and had six children together.) As Roger was fond of saying, we spent the first year three feet apart in our dorm room and the better part of the next thirty-five years a mile apart in Greenwich, Connecticut. He was and is one of my closest friends, as well as the secretary of our Harvard Business School class.

Going to Harvard required a lot of adjustment. Most of my class-mates came from Ivy League schools and from established, distin-guished families. I discovered that I lacked a certain set of social skills that others seemed to have. Although I didn't have a heavy New York accent, I talked fast—*really* fast. I also stuttered a little bit, so I had to learn how to speak more slowly and clearly. (I sometimes still talk too fast!)

In many ways, Harvard was like the navy because my early weeks there were akin to boot camp. I was scared to death when I arrived because I was competing against a student body made up of primar-ily Ivy League–educated men from the top of their classes. In fact, it seemed as though 30 percent of my class had graduated from Princeton. But it was no more intense than anything I'd faced before, including in the navy and in chemical engineering at the University of Rochester. I would quickly discover that I was up to the task.

Everyone joined a study group of six or seven other students. Our group consisted of Roger and me, Art Bellows, Jack Nordeman, Mal Salter, and Jean-Robert Bugnion. Jean-Robert was Swiss and was the group's savant. We all contributed, but his case analysis saved us on many occasions. Our nickname was the Syndicate because of the way we cooperated with one another.

In class, it was great training to sit in a room with ninety other men engaging in what I call mouth-to-mouth combat three times daily. You had to prepare every night, know what you were going to say, and know how to interact with people who were just as prepared as you were.

I must have been good at mouth-to-mouth combat—or maybe I had become used to verbal jousting at a young age—because I did very well my first year.

I spent the summer of 1963 working as a consultant for Union Chimique Belge, a Belgian chemical company founded by Emmanuel

Janssen, whose grandson Daniel Janssen would go on to Harvard Business School and eventually become CEO of UCB. (Daniel worked there as an executive during my tenure at the company and looked after me, ensuring that I was getting an opportunity to contribute.)

For the first half of the summer, I lived in Ghent with a family by the name of Deschamps, who spoke only French and Flemish. Prior to arriving, I spoke no French, so working and living in Belgium allowed me to pick up the language quickly. The family had a son, Jean-Claude, who was around my age and who became a lifelong friend. And Madame Deschamps became my professor savant, dedicated to my daily improvement in French.

UCB manufactured printed linoleums, tablecloths, and other items. In fact, it produced more than 1,500 products, and my job was to conduct an analysis of the business. What could UCB do to make it more profitable and efficient? I wrote a report showing if it reduced the number of products to fewer than two hundred, trimmed its workforce, and updated its equipment, UCB could produce about the same amount of sales and incur a fraction of the expenses.

The company was so pleased with my work that it moved me to the Brussels plant, where I did the same type of analysis. For the second half of the summer, I lived in Brussels and found the city to be a terrific experience. Or, as they say in French, *formidable*.

———————

BY THE END OF THE SUMMER, I had figured out how I was going to afford my second year at Harvard—the only way was to borrow the money. Fortunately, the school loaned me what I needed, so I didn't have to work, which would have interfered with my studies.

Late in my stay in Brussels, my roommate, Roger, had talked me into living off campus with him, Oscar Schafer, Bill Moore, and two Frenchmen, Philippe Sala and Eric Laffont. Roger had rented a big old house called Brown Gables, located in Winchester, Massachusetts, around fifteen miles from the school—twenty minutes by car. He was right about the distance, but as far as the travel time was concerned, it was correct as long as you made the commute at three o'clock in the morning with a police escort! Otherwise, it took much, much longer. That was my first big mistake during my second year.

My second mistake was trying to take six courses when only five were allowed. Being a wise guy, I tried to audit an international economics class, which annoyed the professor. "No one audits my class," he said. I officially signed up for his class and audited another. I think he remembered me anyway. That, coupled with the fact that I was dating a lady who was also dating the graduate student who was marking our papers, somehow got me the lowest grade in my two years in business school. (Well, it's the only excuse I have, anyway.)

I believe that those two mistakes prevented me from graduating with high distinction—also known as becoming a Baker Scholar, an honor awarded to those who graduate in the top 5 percent of the class. I did graduate with distinction, though—that is, in the top 10 percent of my class—which helped with my self-esteem, given my less-than-stellar grades at Rochester.

The year 1963, when I began my second year, was also the year that Harvard Business School recruited twelve women from Radcliffe to join our class. (The following year, they were formally admitted as first-year students.) Although the women had their own "section," I made sure to include them in our social activities—and not just for the reasons you might think. Perhaps it was because I grew up without a mother, but I've always been sensitive to issues of male-female equality in the workplace. I've tried at every point in my career to promote women and give them the same opportunities as men. In any case, my second year at HBS was busy and productive.

During my second year, I became the vice president of the international business club, with the sole responsibility of helping my fellow classmates find jobs overseas. In that capacity, I placed ninety people—a record number at the time—in jobs located everywhere from Switzerland to Yugoslavia. I was also a founder, with Bob Fox, of the small business club, designed to bring small businesses to the campus to recruit students. Everyone knew that HBS graduates were attractive to big companies, but we thought they should be attractive to small companies, too, which had a great deal to offer the graduates as well.

Harvard Business School was then considered the West Point of capitalism. A Harvard MBA supposedly let you write your own ticket in the business world. I thought I could do whatever I wanted when I graduated in 1964. It was true: business school opened my eyes to new possibilities and created a newfound confidence in me. I also collected some great stories and friendships that have lasted a lifetime.

IN THE SPRING OF 1964, my college friend Dave Melnick called to ask me to be the best man at his wedding. Naturally, I said yes. But once I hung up the phone, I realized I didn't have the money to buy a plane ticket to San Francisco, where the wedding was to take place. I raced over to the HBS placement office and asked the woman in charge (who was also a good friend) if there were any companies from California who were interviewing candidates. I didn't care what the job opening was as long as the firm was willing to fly me out to the West Coast. She indicated that there was one company, a Los Angeles firm called Capital Research, whose business was mutual funds. The last thing I was interested in at the time was mutual funds, but I asked if I could get an interview.

She explained that the interview slots were totally booked. But if I came back at four o'clock that day, she suggested, when the last interview was wrapping up, I might be able to talk the chairman of Capital Research, Jim Fullerton, into inviting me to dinner that night. It was traditional for the company doing the hiring to take the interviewees out for a meal, because it provided another opportunity to evaluate the candidates in an informal setting. During this process, around half of the interviewees were usually eliminated from consideration.

In any case, my friend at the placement office thought if I made a good impression at dinner, I might be able to wangle an invitation to California for another interview, which would mean a free plane ticket.

So that's just what I did. At four o'clock, I waited outside the room where the interviews were taking place, and bingo—I had my dinner invitation.

Over the meal, Jim Fullerton said he learned more about me in the fifteen minutes I spent accosting him after his last interview than he did about anyone all day long. Fortunately, I made the cut that night and got the ticket. I guess I needed it more than the other applicants did.

Just before I made my flight arrangements, I received a call from David's mother, who asked if I would travel to San Francisco with "little Barbara," David's sister, who was by then a twenty-year-old senior at the University of Bridgeport, in Connecticut. She was all excited about being the maid of honor at her brother's wedding.

Looking back, I think Mrs. Melnick was in cahoots with Barbara—who, unbeknownst to me, had decided the moment we first met that she was going to marry me. I vaguely remembered meeting her seven years earlier, when I had gone home with David during a holiday break after launching *UGH*. It was that weekend when Barbara notified her family of her intentions toward me. Of course, no one paid much attention to her teenage crush. But Barbara meant it. She was pretty certain of it.

That's Barbara. Extremely determined and very self-assured. "Little Barbara," who really was old enough to make the trip on her own, and I were supposed to meet at the New York airport—Idlewild, now known as John F. Kennedy International Airport. But the last time I had seen her, she was thirteen years old and I was twenty. We didn't exactly recognize each other seven years later.

Apparently, Barbara passed by me more than a few times in the airport while looking for me. I finally had to have her paged over the airport PA system. That did the trick, and at last we were able to find each other and begin our journey.

After we boarded our flight, she talked for a while before she fell asleep with her head resting on my shoulder.

In Hermosa Beach, age eight (1944)

Letters to and from my father

Letters from Mrs. Wellmuth to my father (1946)

PAL NYC runner-up champs (1949)—I'm in the second row, second from the left

As a senior in college, skiing in upstate New York (1957)

At Roosevelt High School, JV city champs (1953)

As Midshipman on USS Albany (1957)

Hawaii (1959)

Our rehearsal dinner, hosted by Aunt Ruth and Uncle Sam (1965)

Kissing Barbara's mother, Mae (1966)

33 Pine Terrace, Demarest, NJ (1967–1969)

With Brad (1969)

G. B. and Barbara at the Montreal Expo (1967)

Family picture, Christmas (1973)

G. B.'s fifth birthday (1971)

With Corey in Vermont (1974)

On vacation (1973)

60 Londonderry Drive, Greenwich, CT (1969–1975)

Surprise trip to Machu Picchu for my fortieth birthday (1976)

Standing in front of the Machu Picchu ruins

Grandpa Harry's seventy-fifth birthday in Arizona (1975)

Ski trip to Vail (1979)

Bermuda (1978)

Family trip to Bermuda with Barbara's parents (1979)

Winter vacation in BVI (1983)

Institutional Investor *magazine picture for story on joining Furman Selz (1983)*

My fiftieth birthday (1986)

Brad's graduation, Brunswick School (1986)

Celebrating Mae's eightieth birthday (1987)

Africa with the Baillie family (1988)

At YPO University, Budapest (1989)

With Tom and Mary Alice O'Malley aboard the Mirabella *(1990)*

Galapagos with the Baillie family (1991)

Barbara's fiftieth birthday (1993)

With my first grandchild, Ra'am,
California (1992)

Nantucket home we built in 1994

With our children (1995) Photo credit: Cary Hazelgrove

BVI (2000)

First meeting with Sophie (1996)

Mae's ninetieth birthday, with Barbara's brother, David (1997)

Patagonia (1998)

*Speaking in Berlin at the Brandenburg Gate for Harvard Business School
International Conference (2000)*

India (2001)

*Visiting Rupa and Rahul Bajaj in India with
the Baillie family (2001)*

Hawaii with G. B. and family (2003)

Vail with our family (2003)

Corey and Jim's wedding (2004)

*Walking Corey down the aisle at her
wedding in Ocean Reef Club, Key Largo (2004)*

I liked the way it felt.

At Dave and Diann's wedding, we danced and drank and had a really fun time. I thought Barbara was very pretty, but too young for me.

After what I considered a terrible interview the following Monday at Capital Research (I was still very hungover and not really all that interested in the job), I returned to Harvard and continued on with my studies. Life as usual went on.

Sort of.

A few days later, I called Barbara and asked her if she would like to spend a weekend at Harvard. She answered yes so quickly it surprised me. I told her I would fix her up with someone her own age but that she could stay at my house.

At the time, she didn't let on that she was really coming to see *me*. She agreed to go out with the guy I fixed her up with, who had strict instructions about the do's and don't's of dating my college friend's little sister. I even gave him a curfew. Then, a few weeks later, I had a problem getting a date of my own for a party, so I called Barbara and asked if she would come and pretend to be my date. Again, much to my surprise, she agreed, and we had a fun but innocent weekend.

BY THIS TIME my father had slowly reemerged in my life, keeping in touch through letters and occasionally sending a few hundred dollars. This contribution was hardly enough to cover my bills or repay the $5,000 student loan I had taken to fund my second year of business school, which at the time seemed like a heavy load. (Starting annual salaries for business-school graduates were on the low side, ranging from $6,000 to $12,000.)

Although my father wanted to attend my Harvard graduation, slated for June of 1964, I didn't invite him. He hadn't shown up for my high school or college graduations, and I didn't want him there when I got my master's degree, either. I simply told him I wasn't planning to walk in the procession with the rest of my class. And I didn't.

As for my prospects after graduation, most of my interviews went very well. In addition to a number of investment banks that made me offers, Capital Research was very interested in me. I guess my interview in Los Angeles went better than I thought it did.

Not knowing that the CEO of Capital Research, Jon Lovelace, was the founder's son, I innocently asked during the interview if there was any nepotism in the firm. Jim Fullerton, the chairman, quickly assured me that although Jon was the founder's son, he had earned the position. Surprise! This question I thought would finish me off. My hunch is that they thought I knew about the family relation from doing research on the company prior to the interview—the sign of a good analyst. A candidate who knew such information would have been impressive because in those days it wasn't so easy to find out things like the CEO's background. I couldn't simply type the company's name into Google. Again, a little bit of luck.

I had some choices to make: if I went the route of investment banking, I would have to start at the lowest level, preparing spreadsheets for a partner and assisting him in other ways—if I was lucky. My instinct told me I'd quickly get restless doing mundane work that wouldn't challenge my problem-solving skills.

During one of my final interviews at a big Wall Street firm, I mentioned that I was thinking of becoming a securities analyst for a mutual fund. The interviewer, who was a senior partner, sat back in his chair, folded his arms over his chest, and then explained that securities analysts are gophers, whereas investment bankers are eagles. *What?*

His characterization, however poetic, did not seem to fit the reality of those jobs. An analyst—a gopher, in his view—gets up in the morning and flies to San Francisco to visit a company, then flies back to his office to write a report. A junior investment banker, the interviewer's so-called eagle, on the other hand, sits in a windowless room with three other junior bankers and waits for someone to give him a task that has to be completed by the next morning.

So much for the metaphor!

In my mind, the Capital Research job was ideal because it required traveling to various companies to research their operations and assess their value. My reports would determine whether or not Capital Research invested in them. I didn't think there would be a better ground floor opportunity or a more effective way to find a company I eventually might run—which was one of my chief goals. Bottom line: I would grab this job even if it meant that other people would think of me as a gopher. It was a risky choice, and I was unprepared for it because I had not taken one single investment course at Harvard. My only experience with stocks was losing money with my Dean Witter account when I was a naval officer.

But from every other point of view, Capital Research was a perfect fit. Plus, they were offering me a starting salary of $11,500, compared to $6,000 at the investment banks. I accepted the offer—I was one of only two people in our class who chose to go to work in mutual funds. Capital also agreed, before I started the job in the fall, that I could go to Central America for the summer to work for INCAE—the Instituto Centroamericano de Administración de Empresas, or Central American Institute of Business Administration. Part of the INCAE program requirement was that participants spend the month of June in Boston taking immersive courses in the Spanish language—eight hours per day! As a result, I became almost fluent.

INCAE had its roots in an initiative spearheaded by John F. Kennedy, who in March of 1963 met with the presidents of Guatemala, El Salvador, Honduras, Nicaragua, and Costa Rica and vowed to assist them in their effort to establish a business school in the region. Kennedy then contacted George P. Baker, dean of the Harvard Business School at the time, who had expressed interest in the initiative. In response, the dean sent three of his professors to Central America to help. One of them was George Cabot Lodge (son of Henry Cabot Lodge Jr.), who was my supervisor that summer.

My responsibility was to write reports about Central American industries, determining which of them presented entrepreneurial opportunities for local businesspeople. We would also write cases that would be taught in the school we were trying to establish. All this was a fantastic experience, especially given that one of my goals was to eventually run my own company. I was on the lookout for companies that I might be able to buy.

Privately, however, I was convinced that my chances for success were limited. For example, at a bar in San Salvador, I met a young lady who was a sales representative for Colgate products. Over dinner she told me how difficult the job was: her territory comprised five countries, an area more than one thousand miles long populated by ten million people. She felt that the market might take many years to develop, if it ever did, and her reasoning seemed sound to me.

However, the business school—nicknamed Harvard South—is now one of the top business schools in Latin America, with a campus in Nicaragua and one in Costa Rica.

I TURNED TWENTY-EIGHT THAT SUMMER, in July. To acknowledge my birthday, my father sent twenty-eight one-dollar bills stuffed into an envelope to my local post office. It was a thoughtful gesture for sure. But when I received it, I ended up with what one would expect—an empty envelope. I suspect its bulging thickness gave away its contents.

I wrote to thank my dad, sharing the story of the missing cash. He became very upset over my not receiving the money. Oddly, he blamed *me*! His moods, and his way of seeing things, were always unexpected. This tense exchange started a period of further separation and anger between us, one that went on for some time.

PART TWO

No Longer Alone

Leaving for our honeymoon (1965)

CHAPTER EIGHT

Her Only and Best-Paying Client

c: 1964–1966

WHEN THE INCAE ASSIGNMENT came to an end, I returned to the United States to start my job, and my new life, at Capital Research, which had been established in 1933. By 1964, it was a fifteen-person business with $350 million under management, the second-largest firm in the mutual fund field.

When I got to Los Angeles, for the first two weeks, I moved in with an HBS classmate, Fred Malek, and his wife, Marlene. During the first week, Fred, who was working for McKinsey at the time, went on a business trip. I was left in his home with Marlene—who happened to be quite attractive. She and I didn't think anything of it, but the neighbors were certainly confused and amused.

Fred—a Vietnam veteran and graduate of West Point who passed away in 2019—went on to have a very distinguished career. He eventually became president of Marriott Hotels and Northwest Airlines, and he was the national finance committee chairman during John McCain's run for president in 2008. Fred and Marlene became great friends of ours, and our families spent a number of vacations together. In 2011, four years before I did, he received the Horatio Alger Award.

After staying with Fred and Marlene, I found a rental house in the Hollywood Hills that overlooked the San Fernando Valley. I shared the house with two classmates from HBS, Art Bellows and Jack Sipes. The woman who rented us the house had what can only be described as a mini-winery in the cellar. She regularly supplied us with freshly made red wine. My original idea was to work for Capital while I tried to find a business to buy. I was in cahoots with four other HBS classmates in this endeavor. We met on weekends once a month. Our plan was to quit our "day jobs" once we found a suitable company. Dreamers—that's what we were.

Initially, this plan seemed realistic, because right from the start, Capital Research allowed me the freedom to do my own thing. It trusted me and gave me autonomy. I wanted and needed to excel as a research analyst, and it provided me with the tools I needed to do that. Though I have often said throughout my career that my choices have not always been based on the amount of money I could make, this was a period of time in my life where making money was quite important to me. I wanted to pay off my student loan as quickly as possible and get out of debt. I also wanted to have some money to invest.

Within three months of arriving in Los Angeles, I found myself on a plane, carrying a briefcase, flying around the United States, talking to lots of very smart people, making contacts, writing reports, and recommending stocks. I was visiting company CEOs and learning how to be an analyst from the best and the brightest on Wall Street. These Wall Street brokerage house analysts were extremely open and helpful: they taught me things I never learned in business school, all about what to look for when buying a stock—price-earnings ratio, book value, cash flow, intellectual property, hidden reserves, and almost anything else that affected the price.

In those days, businesses weren't as secretive as they have to be now. I was welcomed with open arms by the companies I was researching. "What do you want to know?" they would ask. I flew first class, was picked up at the airport, taken out to dinner, and given comprehensive information about their operations. All I had to do was come back and write a report—and decide whether the stock was something we should either buy for our portfolio or sell, if it was already in our portfolio.

I absolutely fell in love with what I was doing, and therefore it didn't take me long to lose interest in buying a business with my would-be investment partner classmates. Besides, we were all driven by conflicting interests and changing circumstances. One of our group of five, Charles Rossotti, had already dropped out. And the other three got interested in a highly leveraged firm that they could buy at what looked like a bargain price, but it was in an industry that didn't seem to have a great future. Nor did it align with one of the foundations of my investment approach, which was finding a theme or a wave that looked like it had a limitless future before others recognized it as a trend. I homed in on themes that interested me for the long term. Eventually I arrived at the theme I wanted to pursue, if I stayed in our little investment group: the recreational vehicle industry.

In 1964, there were only four hundred thousand recreational vehicles in America! A group of Stanford researchers wrote a report predicting that by 1984, there would be four million such vehicles. The manufacturers were almost entirely located in Elkhart, Indiana—and several of them had gone bankrupt. Eureka: I saw an opportunity, but neither my HBS group nor Capital Research (it was too small) was interested, so I bought stock in a company that manufactured RV windows and doors. I paid three dollars per share and sold my stock less than a year later for seven dollars per share. It later went up to $137 per share. Obviously, I sold long before the industry reached its potential—a lesson about patience learned.

I was totally energized by my day job, by the excitement of traveling, and by meeting with highly accomplished business managers and industry analysts. Having such great access to top-notch talent was a real thrill to a kid who grew up in an orphanage. At times, I had to pinch myself to make sure I wasn't dreaming. Was I really getting paid to do such a stimulating and fun job?

I was.

BY THAT POINT, Barbara had graduated from college and had secured a teaching job in Connecticut. When she learned that I was moving to Los Angeles, however, she decided that instead of taking that job, she would likewise move to California. To appear less obvious about her pursuit of me, she applied to San Francisco State University on the pretext of being closer to her brother, David, who was practicing law in San Francisco. Barbara's goal was to pursue a master's degree in counseling. She certainly had the grades, intelligence, and sensitivity for this kind of work and was quickly accepted into the program. (Believe me, her skill has come in very handy over the years, as she has used her training on me many times throughout our marriage. As she always says, I have been her only and best-paying client.)

Over the course of the following year, Barbara and I spent most weekends visiting each other in either Los Angeles or San Francisco. Our relationship quickly became quite close, and I grew to love this woman who was so determined to be my wife.

During our courtship, I learned more about her family. Because of my friendship with David, I already knew that Barbara was born on Staten Island and that her parents owned two stores that sold men's, women's, and children's clothing. The family lived comfortably in a middle-class neighborhood, and the Melnicks' marriage was a happy one.

Mrs. Melnick was a dynamo: she was a buyer for the stores as well as a salesperson, and she handled all the bookkeeping. She had dropped out of high school because she was the oldest in the family and had a responsibility to work, but Barbara thought she could have gone to college or even business school. Mrs. Melnick had a very entrepreneurial nature. Mr. Melnick was a more artistic type who enjoyed arranging the stores' windows. They complemented each other in the best of ways, and Barbara's home life was warm, loving, and stable— exactly the opposite of the way I grew up.

It might come as no surprise, then, that when I shared my feelings for Barbara with my father, he didn't exactly support my decision. In fact, when I told him she and I were getting serious and were planning to get engaged, he said that he was not in favor of my marrying a "Polish Jew!" Hardly the reaction I was hoping for. Instead, he suggested that he had a distant cousin in Paris whom he wanted me to marry. She was Sephardic, born in Egypt. He never could understand anything about me—it was always about what *he* wanted.

It was many years later when I would discover the real reason for his negativity toward Barbara. Not only was Barbara's ethnic background similar to my mother's, but apparently Barbara looked a little like her, too. I suppose it's true that a man grows up and marries his mother—even when he can't possibly be aware of it. But from my father's perspective, even the sight of Barbara triggered in him a memory that was painful to him.

In any case, his overall reaction fit a predictable pattern. He disagreed with almost *everything* I did. After all, he thought I should have stayed in the navy. He thought I should have stayed with my job at Hercules. In some ways, I think he might have been jealous of my success in those early years. When he saw that I had a chance at success in my personal life, he may have become even more envious. Building a happy marriage was something he was never able to do, but it looked like I was going to do it. My father wasn't the only one who wasn't pleased to hear we were engaged. After I proposed to Barbara, at Fort Point, under the Golden Gate Bridge, she visited her brother at his office to tell him the exciting news. When she said, "Ed and I are getting married," his face fell.

"I don't think it's a good idea," he responded. Why? Well, he knew about some of my past: he understood how traumatized I had been by the actions of my father and how living with the foster families and in the orphanages had affected me. And he knew that I carried a lot of anger about it all. He explained to Barbara that I wasn't a simple person, that I came with a lot of emotional baggage. He was afraid Barbara wasn't tough enough to handle me. He wanted her to have a *happier* partner, someone who wasn't as "dark" as I appeared to be.

As I look back on it now, I don't blame him for being concerned. David is an incredibly perceptive guy who was just looking out for his sister. Barbara describes him as being independent from a very young age. He was Phi Beta Kappa, and as I found out later, he received the New York State scholarship that I had applied for in high school and didn't get. He had also been editor in chief of the law review at the University of California law school. Most important, he had his sister's best interests at heart.

Luckily for me, his concerns did not dissuade her.

I will admit, I admired Barbara's fierce determination and independence. In fact, it drew me to her.

WE MARRIED ON AUGUST 8, 1965, at the Melnicks' home on Staten Island. Her father had offered either to pay for a big wedding or to give us $5,000 in cash as a wedding gift. After discussing the pros and cons, Barbara and I opted for the money. My father attended the wedding and, although I feared there might be some kind of a verbal altercation, the ceremony and reception took place without any conflict. As Barbara put it, he was a good soldier. Surprisingly, he got along quite nicely with Barbara's parents.

On the day of our wedding, Barbara's mother had decorated their home from top to bottom with beautiful flowers. She asked me what I thought, and I responded that I thought it looked like a funeral for a bachelor! Not the right thing to say to your new mother-in-law, but eventually, she forgave me.

On our honeymoon, Barbara and I went to the Nassau Beach Club, in the Bahamas, which was the most reasonable resort we could find. Because the only car we had at home was my Karmann Ghia, which had a standard transmission, when we were in the Bahamas I rented a car with a standard transmission so I could teach her how to drive it. Not the best way to start a marriage!

UNTIL I MET BARBARA, I didn't understand the true meaning of desire or love. She says she fell in love with me on the first day we met, without knowing anything about me. Before we married, I sat down and told her some things about me—stuff I had never revealed to anyone about my past. She was the only woman I ever shared my history with, and even then, I didn't tell her everything. It all came out over time, though, slowly and in pieces. And still she continues to love me unconditionally for who I am, flaws and all. In fact, there was absolutely nothing I could have disclosed that would have changed how she felt. If that one thing does exist, I haven't found it . . . yet.

Barbara's love was unconditional, the first time I had ever felt such a thing. To this day, she encourages me to do the right thing, whether it's something small, like standing up straight, or something big, like following my conscience. I have never experienced her type of acceptance before or since. Since the day we said "I do," I have liked how she always makes me feel. And I still do.

Holding our firstborn, G. B. (1966)

CHAPTER NINE

Hit the Go Button

c. 1966–1971

IN SEPTEMBER OF 1966, Capital Research asked me to run its
New York office, which seemed crazy of the company at the time,
putting an entire operation in the hands of a thirty-year-old. After
all, I had been there for only two years. But I guess no one else wanted
the job.

After some hesitation, I said yes. It meant a move back East, but it
was an opportunity like no other: I was going to be the New York representative of the second-largest mutual fund company in the United
States! The office was located on the fifty-seventh floor of the Chase
Manhattan building. As I recall, David Rockefeller himself had his
office on the fifty-eighth floor.

At that point, Barbara and I became parents for the first time. We
had a son we named Geoffrey Blair Hajim, who quickly became known
as G. B. When we made the decision to go to New York, Barbara was
just one course shy of completing her master's degree, and we both
agreed that she should graduate before she moved to the East Coast.

I wanted to support Barbara in every way I could and certainly
didn't want to be *that* husband—the one who considers his career more
important that his wife's. We were in a partnership and had set out to
pursue our collective dream as one.

Barbara entrusted me with the task of finding an apartment in San Francisco for her and G. B. to live in for two months while she finished school. It wasn't as easy as we thought it would be. After seeing every short-term rental that was available in the city, I discovered that no one wanted to rent to a young man who was going to deposit his wife and small son in the apartment and then leave. As much as I tried to explain our circumstances, it must have sounded to most real estate agents like abandonment. Finally, I found a nice apartment that would take us. The sticking point was that it was in the middle of Haight-Ashbury. Of course, today, that wouldn't be an issue, but back then, it was the epicenter of San Francisco's hippie revolution, the time of "turn on, tune in, drop out." But all that barely registered with Barbara. Thankfully, her attitude then, as it is to this day, was to simply do what has to be done. She's very adaptable, which is a great trait in anyone.

I was quite concerned about the separation from Barbara and G. B. But my boss at Capital Research told me I could fly back and forth every other weekend to be with them, which was comforting to Barbara and me. But in the summer of 1966, the airline machinists' union went on strike, affecting five carriers nationwide and shutting down 60 percent of the industry. The strike lasted forty-three days, so I didn't get to see my family for most of the summer.

Fortunately, by the time Barbara graduated, the strike had ended. I flew to San Francisco, we packed up our car, and drove across the country with our baby boy. We had a great time driving in Barbara's gray Plymouth Valiant convertible. The car had no seat belts—they didn't become mandatory until 1968. Nor were there any car seats back then, so we improvised: G. B. rode in a bassinet in the backseat.

During one stopover in Alberta's Jasper National Park, in the Canadian Rockies, we had a moment of excitement after a family of bears shredded our convertible's roof looking for food while we slept. (Perhaps we should never have taken this detour, but I've always had a touch of wanderlust.) In any case, we survived and traveled roofless to Edmonton, where we had the entire assembly temporarily repaired with white tape. We must have been quite a sight on the highway for the rest of the trip.

Early that summer I had found a house to rent at 6 Churchill Road in Englewood Cliffs, New Jersey. It was the only thing we could afford at the time, because living in Manhattan was out of our financial reach. The owners of the house, Dr. and Mrs. Bernstein, were leaving for London and looking for a nice quiet couple with no pets. We filled the bill, so we got a great deal on the place. Ever the trouper, Barbara put up with living in a neighborhood where she didn't know another soul, yet all the while she supported me through my career transition.

I commuted daily from New Jersey to downtown Manhattan, but the trip was made easier because the owner of the house persuaded our next-door neighbor to drive me one way in the mornings. In the evenings, I would either take the subway and bus home or Barbara would drive into the city with the little guy and pick me up.

A year later we bought a large house with a pool at 33 Pine Terrace in Demarest, New Jersey, just a few towns north of Englewood Cliffs. Though it meant a slightly longer commute for me, it was worth it. The price was $78,000, though it wasn't exactly move-in ready. In fact, the house needed a lot of work—there was a big crack in the living-room wall. Honestly, we never did fix it, nor did we ever completely furnish the living room. Our mortgage payments were high, and it wasn't our top priority.

In the summer of 1968, when our second son was about to be born, my father wrote and said he wanted to drive up from his home in Hollywood, Florida, to be with us for the birth. Though I had written him often over the years to keep him up to date on our life, because of his feelings toward Barbara, we hadn't seen much of him.

Over the years, Barbara did the best she could to try to repair the relationship between my father and me. She couldn't understand it because her upbringing had been so different. To her, a father was a loving presence. Parents were people who did everything they possibly could for their children. The idea of taking off and leaving a child with strangers would never have occurred to her parents. Yet she told me that she wasn't angry at my father for the way he had treated me when I was a child. But she was hurt—hurt on *my* behalf. She tried her best, but the relationship between my father and me never got much better than the cordial but distant rapport we shared.

Still, Barbara and I discussed his genuine interest in connecting with us. We decided to ask him to join us for our son's birth. But when my father arrived, it looked like Barbara might not have the baby for another week or more. So he stayed with us for a couple of days before impulsively deciding to drive to California and back again before the due date. We couldn't imagine why he would want to do this. At age sixty-eight, why go to all the trouble? The only explanation that occurs to us in hindsight is that he loved his car and loved to drive. In fact, his car was his most prized possession—it was like his horse. In a way, he couldn't sit still.

So that's what he did. When he came back from California, he was in time for the birth of our son Jon Bradley Hajim, whom we call Brad. It was one of the best visits we all shared, filled with celebration and the sound of babies. I don't think I had ever seen my father have such a good time. Everything ended on a high note. But after he left, we went back to our old ways, remaining somewhat estranged and living in what I would call a peaceable coexistence.

I ABSOLUTELY LOVED MY NEW JOB and thrived in it. I worked very hard, and it paid off.

I'm sure luck had a lot to do with it, but I had two fantastic years, in '67 and '68. Some of the client accounts I managed increased in value by more than 100 percent, which in turn helped us attract new accounts. In 1967, I significantly outperformed the market and received a $70,000 bonus. But I wasn't particularly happy about it, because I thought it should have been even more. As I pointed out to my bosses, I reckoned my stock selections were responsible for between 40 and 50 percent of the company's performance. Another sign of my unnecessary impatience.

Three short years after being hired, I was made a vice president and became a shareholder in the company. Senior management also put me on their strategic planning committee, which was just being established. They thought I would be good at arranging meetings, but I had other ideas. Because strategy was my favorite subject, I was thinking out of the box from the start.

I immediately joined a few other voices (mainly that of Ned Bailey, one of the firm's senior officers), saying that we should expand our market from individuals (our main market at the time) to institutions such as corporate pension funds and endowments. I also became a zealot about expanding our product line from just growth-with-income funds and income-with-growth funds to funds that solely focused on growth and funds that focused solely on income.

The first goal was completed with the formation of the Capital Guardian Trust Company as a subsidiary of Capital Research. Ned Bailey was appointed to head it up, and I was made the portfolio manager as well as a shareholder.

At the same time, I continued to pursue the second goal—the broadening of our product line to include separate growth and income funds. These would serve as bookends to our growth-with-income and income-with-growth funds and go a long way toward helping us complete our product line and thus better position ourselves against our competitors.

After many proposals, the company agreed to my plan but did not want these types of funds to be part of the Los Angeles operation. I suggested that we form a new subsidiary, similar to the Capital Guardian Trust Company, to pursue this strategy and locate it on the East Coast.

Finally, after a year of negotiations, the company acquiesced (I got its backing but not necessarily everyone's blessing) and let me create my own mutual fund company. This was what I loved most—starting things from scratch. I was almost convinced I couldn't fail—and that arrogance was a real weakness.

Capital agreed that the new company could be located in Greenwich, Connecticut, where I would also be living. We started Greenwich

Management Company, named for its location, in 1969 with $1 million in capital. Capital Research put up $700,000 of that, and I put up $300,000. Capital Research owned 70 percent of the company, and I owned 30 percent.

My first partner was Steve Reynolds, a former colleague from Capital Research who came with me to help launch this dream. We rented four hundred square feet of undivided, open office space in the back of a bowling alley with just one window overlooking a dingy, weed-strewn area. Feeling as though we needed our own work spaces, Steve spent one entire night painting modular office partitions at a local company; as payment, it gave us a couple of them for our offices. We hired a secretary to do the day-to-day stuff and hit the go button.

In the meantime, Barbara and I sold our home in Demarest, New Jersey, and moved to Greenwich. We felt that being in southwestern Fairfield County was the perfect location for our family because it had good schools and low taxes. We found a half-built house on two acres adjacent to a pond on Londonderry Drive, in a great neighborhood. The contractor had the house on the market for $105,000, a real bargain. Because we sold our house in New Jersey for $97,000, it wasn't a giant financial leap to move into our new three-bedroom oasis, even after we built a pool.

TODAY, I ALWAYS TELL PEOPLE never to start a company from the ground up. Instead, always find a platform—an organization that already has an established business and client base—from which to launch it. How did I learn this? By starting the Greenwich Management Company! We certainly had no platform—and no money under management. We were just a few people in a four-hundred-square-foot room. The enterprise had, shall we say, disaster written all over it.

When you're starting from scratch, multiple things can go wrong that are impossible to anticipate. But I was still rather naive and didn't realize that back then. All I had was a lot of chutzpah and the belief that

I could succeed by replicating what I had done for the previous five years. What I didn't understand was that when you're in an established company (like Capital Research) that employs the best people in the business and offers an excellent and experienced team to help you, it's easier to be good at what you do.

My immediate priority at Greenwich Management was finding some real money to invest. Fortunately, shortly after we launched, I found a little fund in New Jersey that the SEC was unhappy with called the Growth Fund of America. The fund's board was looking for a way to get out. Given our pedigree, as part of Capital Research, it was easy to see why we should take it over. What's more, the name Growth Fund of America seemed like divine intervention: Capital Research's largest fund, founded in 1933, was called the Investment Company of America. It just felt like it was meant to be.

We bought the troubled fund, which had only $500,000 in assets, for $50,000 plus $50,000 in legal fees. We put together an impressive board for such a tiny fund: Bob Egelston, president of the Capital Group, the parent company of Capital Research; Ted Nierenberg, president of Dansk International Designs; Bob Smith, a director of the Singer Company; Robert Plumb Jr., treasurer of the American Smelting and Refining Company; Hugo Uyterhoeven, professor at the Harvard Business School; and Bob Fox, senior vice president of Canada Dry— the same Bob Fox with whom I had founded the small business club at Harvard Business School.

Six months later, we added a trader, Gil Baird, and a COO, Bob Davies, and moved our offices into a space in the new Greenwich Plaza at a whopping five dollars a square foot.

In 1971, we completed our mission by launching an income fund, which we called the Income Fund of America. We raised $30 million for it through an underwriting executed by Dean Witter and White Weld & Company. It was the second-largest fund offering in the country that year.

We also had secured the name Bond Fund of America for our next offering. I had put a hedge-fund fee on the Growth Fund of America

(1 percent of the fund's net asset value, plus 20 percent of the profits), the first and maybe only such fee in the industry at the time. We were ahead of our time, but the SEC disallowed it after that year. (The SEC regulation should be called the Growth Fund of America Rule.)

The first three years were glorious! We proved ourselves to be one of the best-performing fund managers in the country. In fact, by 1971, the Growth Fund of America was the third-best-performing fund out of six hundred in the business. We grew the company to twenty-five employees and managed $150 million in assets. Money started rolling in. As a result, I became a little full of myself. I actually thought I could manage the fund, market the fund, and manage the people, too.

A classic mistake.

You have to be cautious when you leave a mature organization and believe that your fledgling operation will perfectly emulate the parent group. You will quickly find out how important your past processes and partners were to your success. Our little company began generating 25 percent of Capital Research's total sales, which disturbed some people in Los Angeles—mainly those who were not supportive of my forming Greenwich Management from the start.

Remember, I got the company's *backing* but not everyone's *blessing*. They'd been in business for thirty-five years, and Greenwich Management had been in existence for only three. I could see there was a lot of unhappiness, and it resulted in Capital Research deciding that we would no longer be able to use its sales force. When that happened, we had to find other ways to raise funds.

Undeterred, we decided to market our investment management service to the corporate pension fund community. I went on the road and, using our three-year record and the Capital Research reputation as leverage, landed a number of corporate clients. These efforts propelled our growth forward, though they added a whole new dimension to our marketing requirements.

Our young family (Christmas, 1972)

CHAPTER TEN

The Question I Would Have Asked

c. 1971–1974

I N THE MIDDLE OF 1971, which would turn out to be a stressful and life-altering year, I received a phone call that no son wants to get. On June 1, 1971, my father had a heart attack and died. This sudden and shocking news came just three days before his seventy-first birthday.

Hearing that my father was gone hit me very hard for many reasons. To be certain, it came as a complete surprise, since he appeared to be quite healthy when I had last seen him. He exercised on a regular basis and was careful with his diet, though he did consume quite a bit of sugar, adding spoonfuls of it to his coffee. He also smoked early on in his life and never liked going to doctors for regular checkups. My guess is that he must have had an undiagnosed heart condition.

But there was another, more subtle reason that may have contributed to my father's death. As I've said before, my father's car was his most prized possession—and this goes for every car he owned. His freedom to drive was almost synonymous with his identity as a person. But I later learned that, in the year before he died, he had gotten into a number of fender benders. He had also been given multiple traffic tickets. In fact, things had reached the point where it looked like he might lose his license altogether.

I believe that the emotional strain of all this—the prospect that he might not be able to drive—adversely affected his mental and physical health. In a sense, he lived for his car; without it he felt incomplete.

In fact, when the heart attack occurred, my father was behind the wheel. Apparently, he stopped the car, then he had the attack. He died almost instantly.

My father, who stopped working in his sixties, had been living from hand to mouth for the last several years of his life. To make ends meet, he would take odd jobs here and there—fixing radios, anything he could do—just to make a little cash. I offered to help him financially many times, but he would never accept it. I think he was too proud to take money from me.

Despite our estrangement, my father's death came as a terrible blow. He had been the only family I'd known my entire life. And despite our troubled relationship, I always knew that he loved me. I thought back to all the disappointment and grief we had shared over the years—particularly one conversation we had when he visited us in Connecticut in 1969, after we first moved there.

I'd told him about Greenwich Management and its great success. Instead of letting me know how happy he was for me, or how proud, he said, "I no longer understand you or what you're doing." What? Obviously, he was resentful and jealous—truly tragic, because most parents feel proud of their children when they excel. But my father was battling demons.

It dawned on me after his death that we would never reconcile, because any opportunity for doing so had passed and would never come again. I never would have closure.

There are many things I would have wanted to say to my father had he lived longer. I would have asked him *why*—*why did you take me away from my mother? Why did you tell me she was dead? What really went on between the two of you?*

I desperately wanted him to understand that his life and mine were different. I had taken a different path. I had made different choices. And I wanted him to respect them. I also wanted him to accept Barbara, which he never fully did. He didn't outright reject her, but he never completely embraced her as part of the family.

Most of all, I wanted him to know that no matter what had happened to us, no matter what he did to me, I still loved him.

As I've said, throughout my life, I've carried a lot of anger about my childhood circumstances and the way my father handled his parental role. Yes, he had a difficult personality. And it wasn't just me he had trouble with. While I was writing this book, I discovered a new piece of history. In March of 1936, just before I was born, my father testified at a congressional hearing about aviation safety. As part of his testimony, he referred to yet another job failure, his "removal for cause from the position of assistant airways keeper in the Bureau of Commerce" in Atlanta. In this statement, he accused at least one coworker of anti-Semitism. It's painful for me to read about these kinds of incidents. I'm still not sure how much more I want to know about them.

Shortly after my father died, I finally went to a therapist, the wonderful Peggy Penn at the Ackerman Institute, to try to deal with my feelings and resolve them in a healthful way. She suggested that I write letters to my father as if he were still alive. I would then answer them myself, putting myself in his shoes, writing from his perspective. That actually helped a lot, allowing me to be totally honest about how I was feeling and why. I could also see things from his point of view. By doing this exercise, I realized that I could have tried harder to establish a better relationship with him. I could have done a lot of things differently, but I didn't. One thing that always stopped me was my anger toward him. I felt sad and angry with myself, although I no longer harbored any animosity toward my father. Long ago, I had decided to get on with my life. I had a new company, a loving wife, two children—with a third on the way—and was living in a new community, where I was making good friends.

After my father's death, as difficult as it was, I went to Florida with Barbara and her mother, Mae, to settle my father's affairs. When we entered his apartment, to my astonishment, I saw that he had a Harvard pennant mounted on the wall! A few of his acquaintances told me that he often bragged about me. Ah . . . so he must have been prouder of me than he let on.

Thank God for Mae, because she handled many of the difficult details I simply could not face. We found a cemetery, and I bought a double-size plot in a gated-off section of the grounds. I suppose I was trying to give him something he did not have in life and relieve some of my guilt in the process. At least he would have a final resting place that set him apart.

We placed an obituary in the local newspaper and held a ceremony at his graveside. A few people showed up, but not as many as I had hoped. After that day, I spent long hours thinking about my father and my relationship with him. As I discovered, he had left very little behind except a suitcase full of letters, mostly those from me. After opening it and looking inside, I quickly closed it up. I shipped it back to Greenwich and put it in a closet in our home.

"Someday I will come back to this," I thought. I wasn't in a big hurry to revisit the contents of that suitcase.

———————

AFTER I MOURNED THE DEATH OF MY FATHER, a happier day came toward the end of 1971. On December 30, Barbara and I experienced the circle of life and the joys of parenthood for the third and final time when she gave birth to a baby girl. I witnessed the whole thing, something I will never forget. We named our beautiful strawberry-blond, blue-eyed baby Corey Brooke Hajim. We were all overjoyed by her arrival. It was a dream to have a girl and a sister for our two boys. The house was more filled than ever with young energy and our high hopes for the future.

As this tumultuous year ended, Greenwich Management Company was still riding high. We had an outstanding three-year record and some excellent institutional accounts. We even had a small account with a Swiss bank, which had the potential to get much bigger if we did well.

But because of the loss of Capital Research's marketing and distribution services, the nature of my job changed. I went from concentrating on one thing—managing the portfolio—to doing three things at once: managing the portfolio; marketing to our individual shareholders as well as our institutional clients, both foreign and domestic; and managing a staff of twenty-five people.

The institutional clients were particularly difficult, because in those days they required four meetings per year. You had to be fully prepared when facing a corporate pension fund committee, and each one had its own needs. We had *five* institutional clients, so this translated to twenty meetings per year in five different locations.

At the age of thirty-six, I believed I could do almost anything and was out to prove it. I might have even made it work, since I was aware of the challenges. But 1972 would turn out to be a year in which the Capital Research investment philosophy was turned on its head.

The Capital Research method, which I fully embraced, was to buy value stocks that had low price-earnings multiples. In 1972, though, the "favorite fifty"—fifty of the biggest and highest-quality stocks, which had high price-earnings multiples—went up while the rest of the market went down. That included the small stocks in which Greenwich Management specialized. Those stocks were our forte, and they were, unfortunately, especially hard hit. Therefore, while the market indexes, driven by these large stocks, were up, we were down.

Our clients started to redeem. (Capital Research had similar problems with its Capital Guardian Trust Company, losing about half its assets to the big banks as those banks were heavily invested in the "favorite fifty.") Greenwich Management had three very good years, but we had not accumulated enough capital to cushion a down market and serious redemptions. In addition, I had to worry about the staff that I had hired: their well-being came first.

This was a painful but important lesson: you can't effectively manage money, market its products, *and* manage people. It's just too much.

In other fields, it's easy to understand this maxim. For example, you can't be a neurosurgeon, a dermatologist, and a podiatrist at the same time. Each requires a different skill set. Right there and then, I learned that to be truly effective, I had to focus on *one* of those areas if I wanted to be the best at it.

This lesson was tough and eventually cost me the company.

In retrospect, perhaps I had failed my employees and everyone who supported me by trying to wear too many hats.

In 1973 Capital Research called and said, "This business isn't working. Why don't you sell Greenwich Management back to us? You can stay on and continue working for Capital Research. You'll be seen as a hero for the niche you've created." It offered to buy the company back for exactly what I paid for it.

I was feeling particularly bearish, so I decided, with the agreement of my board, to sell my interest back.

When all was said and done, I heard a lot of variations of "I told you so" from some of the original naysayers. Some of the people in Los Angeles hadn't liked what I was doing from the start. Some thought I was destroying the culture of the firm. In a sense, this was their vindication. So be it.

As soon as I signed the papers selling back my shares, my heart told me that my relationship with Capital Research would never be the same. You have to listen to those inner voices when they talk to you, providing clues to the future for sure!

The company ceremoniously dangled a carrot in front of me, promising me that the status quo would prevail. But in my gut, I knew it wouldn't. Besides, it didn't feel like it was the right move to go back to Los Angeles. In short, I wasn't excited about staying with the company, and Barbara wasn't thrilled with the idea, either. She had flown out to California several times to try to find a home for our family—without success. In the end, we had made a very nice life in Connecticut. Since our family was our top priority, it didn't make sense to disrupt our lives to move to a city for a job I no longer wanted. Sometimes you need to know when a partnership has run its course. And sometimes, it's better to sever ties and leave on your own, even if the next step is unknown. That's often the road less traveled, but it's so worth the journey.

In any case, I eventually felt unwelcome at Capital Research. Though that realization hurt, I felt grateful for all I had been given. My bosses taught me everything I knew and allowed me to spread my wings in ways I could never have imagined. I was given equal opportunity to succeed and to fail. I did both, and learned a tremendous amount from these experiences.

I decided that the best course of action was to resign from Capital Research. So that's exactly what I did. Fortunately, Jim Fullerton, Capital's chairman, and Bob Egelston, its president, took the news very well, even though they had always supported me and genuinely wanted me to stay. As it turned out, Capital Research did an excellent job managing both the Growth Fund of America (which at one time was the largest equity fund in the business, with more than $150 billion in assets) and the Income Fund of America (which reached $80 billion in assets).

I didn't have many mentors in my life, but throughout the years I kept in touch with Jim Fullerton, who stood behind me all the way, not only during my time with the company but also well past my leaving. He did everything he could to guide me, right up until he died, at the age of ninety-eight.

For example, Jim taught me to always use humor when giving a speech and to explain the history behind what I was talking about and why it mattered. He was what I always refer to as a *practical intellectual*. He never made anyone feel inadequate, because he was able to articulate things in a straightforward, understandable way with a hint of humor. I sometimes wonder how many lives Jim touched over the years, and if he realized the profound impact he had on others.

I sure hope so.

Before finalizing my departure from Capital Research, I had to sell my holdings in the parent company stock, which in the long run amounted to a huge loss. Capital today is worth many thousands of times what it was worth in 1974, when it had $4 billion under management. As of 2020, it manages more than $1.5 *trillion*. In retrospect, I probably should have toughed it out, scaled back the company, and stayed in business with them.

I always wonder: if I had been better financed, or if my father had not lost everything in 1929, or if he hadn't died in 1971, could I have gone on and built a major money-management company? Ah, the what-ifs!

As I see it, my experience demonstrates that the ability to pick yourself up after you have fallen is one of the great secrets of success. It also proves that a bend in the road is not the end of the road.

*Fox Lair—21 Guinea Road,
Greenwich, CT (1975–2002)*

CHAPTER ELEVEN

Transform or Perish

c. 1974–1977

A S LUCK WOULD HAVE IT, while things were unraveling with Capital Research and Greenwich Management, I ran into Bob Fomon, the CEO of E. F. Hutton, at a wedding. When I told him what was happening with my job situation, he shrugged it off and said, "Forget about that mutual fund business. Come to work for me."

You cannot plan for moments like these, but you do have to be willing to take the chance when it presents itself. As fate would have it, a new partner came along at just the right time.

In those days, E. F. Hutton was the second-largest retail brokerage in the industry (a retail brokerage is one that caters to individuals rather than to institutional clients). It was also considered the best. And although I did need to work, I didn't want to take just any job after leaving Capital Research.

One of the reasons Hutton appealed to me was that Bob wanted the firm to excel on the institutional side as well as in the retail business. He was eager to hire me, too, because at the time, there were not many people in the brokerage industry who knew the institutional market. Why not hire an experienced portfolio manager to handle it?

Even though I had been on what we call the "buy side" of the business, whereas Hutton was on the "sell side," the move fit Bob's instinctive method of management perfectly. I believed Hutton was a company with an A-list of customers that had not been well serviced. I saw the job as an opportunity to prove what I could do.

After some negotiation, I accepted a position as a senior vice president at the firm. At the time, the industry—"the Street," in familiar parlance—considered my coming on at Hutton just another failed effort by a big retail house to get into the institutional business. In fact, most of Hutton's major competitors believed we wouldn't succeed. But Bob and I were determined to prove them all wrong.

I made the transition to Hutton in September of 1974, which I felt was at, or close to, the bottom of the market. Hutton's stock price had declined to two dollars per share, its lowest in history. But in retrospect, I entered the brokerage business at exactly the right time, because the institutional business was just starting to become viable as institutions began to grow rapidly. There were a number of research boutiques that were becoming significant players, but the big houses hadn't really entered the business yet. Volume was low, and commissions were generous.

When Bob offered me the job, he said I would be taking over from the person who had the job before me, a man who was responsible for the sales and research side of the institutional business. His responsibility encompassed only a limited number of large institutional accounts. But I knew that in order to be successful, we had to put all three functions—sales, research, and trading—under one manager (meaning me) and place all or most of the firm's institutional accounts, wherever they were located in the country, under the same umbrella.

I told Bob that we couldn't do what he wanted unless he made these changes, which required him to break some internal glass. This meant taking some responsibility away from people who had had it for a long time and who wanted to keep it. For example, Bob took trading away from the head of that division, which did not endear me to that man at all. He also pulled most of the institutional accounts from the powerful regional directors, which did not make me too popular with them, either, because their brokers would lose these big accounts to my new division.

Bob and I knew that these accounts were not being serviced the way they had to be to get the commission flow they could potentially produce. He agreed that my strategy would and should be put in place going forward, especially because that structure was employed by some of the investment banks that concentrated exclusively on the institutional side. If it worked for them, it should work for us.

The first thing I did was call my team together. I told them there would be a meeting at 7:30 each morning that they were expected to attend. I wanted everyone to know that we were serious about this business no matter what others thought. I told them our numbers would do the talking.

To prove my point, the next thing I did was hire a top professional from Goldman Sachs, an all-star analyst named Bowen Smith, who was an expert in the paper industry. (A so-called all-star analyst is one who has been highly ranked by *Institutional Investor* magazine.) Yes, as hard as that may have been to believe at the time, Hutton successfully hired someone away from Goldman Sachs! I wanted to send a message, and that hire did it.

I ALWAYS ADVISE PEOPLE who are considering a job opportunity to make sure they understand how that position is supposed to make money for the company and what or who determines whether that effort is successful. I tell them to try to secure responsibility for their own P&L and oversee it closely. That's what I did, and that's probably why I got off to a good start.

As luck would have it, Washington and the SEC were about to change the commission system from one of fixed rates, which had been in place from the beginning of time, to negotiated rates, which everyone knew meant lower commissions.

At the time, many all-star analysts worked for boutique investment banks that handled only research, or only research and sales, and had no trading capability. Clients would direct their trades through major brokers like Hutton, who would, in turn, pay the boutiques for their services. These were called directed commissions. With the ending of fixed rates on May 1, 1975, just eight months after I took over Hutton's institutional effort, there was little room for the system of directed commissions to boutique firms.

This change was called May Day—and indeed it was a kind of Mayday for the boutiques, because their commissions dropped precipitously. (Six months later, Samuel L. Hayes, a professor at the Harvard Business School, wrote a case study about Hutton's and my response to May Day that was taught as part of the finance curriculum.)[3]

As the boutiques got in trouble because of declining revenues, I quickly moved to offer their all-star analysts jobs at Hutton. Given the 1974 bear market and May Day, the acquisition costs were quite low. For example, in one transaction, we acquired three top analysts (Denny Leibowitz, Bob Cornell, and David Taylor) from Black and Company for a total salary of $100,000 plus production-based incentives. I repeated this tactic a number of times, and we quickly built a great team.

I also recruited Mike Sherman, who was a top-rated money manager and an erudite and articulate observer and writer on both the economy and the stock market. Together we became the company's market strategy team (he did most of the work). With everything in place, institutions started to believe in our commitment to their business. We added salesmen and traders, and it felt as if I was on my way again. We suddenly went from having no position on the all-star list to being one of the top three firms, which virtually required the institutions to pay attention to us.

I also won over the regional directors, because the research and prestige of our all-star analysts helped their retail brokers get more business. The one thing I did not do is win over the trading department. In

---

[3] See "E. F. Hutton and Co. (B)" and "E. F. Hutton and Co. (C)" (October 1975; case numbers 9–276–109 and 9–276–110).

its eyes, someone with the kind of professional experience I had could never understand how to run a trading department.

By 1976, business was flourishing. Although Bob had the foresight to put an institutional effort in place, he did not want it to affect Hutton's mother lode, which was the retail business. On that note, one morning he called and reminded me that we had another business at Hutton, one that still generated "90 percent of the revenues"—the retail business—and it was starting to be negatively affected by the existence of our lower commissions.

"Ed, you've done enough. You can now take over retail," he said at one of our regular morning sessions in his office. He was praising me for a job almost too well done. He wanted me to start thinking about retail so he could promote George Ball to president. George was always the other person in Bob's office for every morning planning session.

I was flattered, but I had a different idea. George knew the retail business well, which I did not. Also, it appeared Bob was desperate to build up his banking business, which I felt needed a lot of work. My concept was to have my highly respected research analysts work with Hutton's bankers to generate more business. I also wanted the trading department to better service its banking clients. This seemed like the logical next step for my twenty-five all-star analysts. As I explained it to Bob, I felt that analysts knew more about industries and companies than many bankers did. I also felt that it is what corporate clients wanted as the good-old-boy, old-school-tie style of banking was on the wane. I furthermore believed that offering potential banking clients research, institutional following, and trading was the wave of the future. As I did often in my career, I was trying to look forward, asking, "What's next?"

Unfortunately, Bob disagreed with my idea. He kind of looked down on analysts as a lesser species and didn't see the connection between either research and banking or trading and banking. He saw bankers as client people and analysts as people who crunched numbers and recommended stocks. I believe this is one of the things that led to the firm's downfall and, ultimately, to its sale to Shearson at a bargain price ten years later.

DURING THE EARLY 1970S, things on the home front were going very well. Barbara and I were very happy on Londonderry Drive and never intended to move. But one day, out of the blue, she got a call from her friend Judy Steinhardt, who was real-estate hunting for herself. She asked Barbara to come along to help.

Well, you know what happened. Judy didn't buy *anything*, but Barbara came home all excited about a gorgeous French country home on eight acres called Fox Lair, just two blocks from Londonderry Drive. It came complete with a pool, was on a pond, and backed up to a nature preserve—the works. When Barbara told me that we had to see it, I thought she was crazy, especially after hearing the listing price! No way we could afford it. However, she was convinced it was the ideal home for our family.

As usual, her patience and determination paid off. Over time, the price kept coming down, as did the price of all real estate at that time. (In 1974 and '75, real estate crashed in New York and Connecticut.) Then one of the owners died and the other closed the house, leaving it empty. A year later, it was put up for sale to settle the estate. Phil Drake, a lawyer friend, phoned us and said that the price had been cut by two-thirds: were we interested?

Thrilled, we decided to buy Fox Lair even though we couldn't sell our house on Londonderry Drive. We also knew that Fox Lair needed work. For one thing, it was full of mildew—but we were ready to tackle it because once it was cleaned up, it would be perfect for us.

As Barbara said, it only took a year and around a thousand gallons of Clorox and six thousand gallons of white paint to make it livable. And fortunately, just before we moved into our dream home, the house on Londonderry did sell, making us more comfortable financially. As it turned out, we would remain at Fox Lair for the following twenty-seven years.

It really was the ideal home for us. It had four bedrooms and five baths upstairs and a lovely guest room on the first floor that we called

Grandma's room. Even the basement was wonderful—there was a large area down there that we called the cat room because it had a little door that the cat could go in and out of all by herself.

The concrete walls in the basement were painted red, and it became the preferred hangout for the kids and their friends. We always encouraged the kids to have their friends over, and Barbara made sure our refrigerator was well stocked at all times. Plus she always had a tray of cookies or muffins sitting on the kitchen counter. (A habit she still continues.) Once, she found a note on the refrigerator from one of Brad's friends telling us that we had run out of chocolate ice cream! Another time, after coming home from a family dinner, we found Brad's best friend, Bart Osman, in the cat room watching TV and drinking a bottle of beer! He knew where our house key was hidden.

THE ONLY CONSTANT IN LIFE IS CHANGE. People change and businesses change. If you don't adapt, you will not survive. After all, when you see a change, you are rarely, if ever, the *only* one seeing it. I tell young entrepreneurs to take the lead if at all possible, because there is a huge advantage to being a first mover. The late businessman Andrew Grove focused on this idea in his book *Only the Paranoid Survive: How to Exploit the Crisis Points That Challenge Every Company*. I believe it's one of the best books ever written about business.

In 1976, institutional brokerage was beginning to emerge as a strong force in the economy, and I perceived that it could become as or more important than retail brokerage. Hutton had to transform or perish.

Indeed, while Hutton and I were arguing over the direction of the business, other firms, including Lehman Brothers, were sensing a change in the air, plotting to enter institutional brokerage in a big way, too. And because there were very few people who had my experience or success in that field, I became a person of interest to anyone wanting to enter or build the institutional business. To firms that needed someone with sales and research knowledge, I was a prime candidate ripe for the picking.

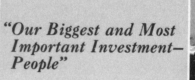

"*Our Biggest and Most Important Investment—People*"

Lehman Brothers (1979)

CHAPTER TWELVE

The Hornet's Nest

c. 1977–1980

I SPENT THREE YEARS AT E. F. HUTTON and did exactly what the firm needed me to do. As a result, my time there gave me my "postdoctoral" training in the brokerage business and really taught me how to run a company—through hands-on experience. My team and I had transformed the institutional department at Hutton, putting it on the map.

But I wasn't successful in convincing Bob or my other Hutton colleagues of the coming changes in the industry. While I was busy trying to show them which way the wind was blowing, my success in the institutional business had caught the attention of some other houses, who called me to see if I was interested in leaving Hutton. Initially, I wasn't. I loved my newly built institutional team. Besides, Bob and I were friends, as were his wife, Sharon, and Barbara. Unfortunately, I disagreed with his strategy, which, to me, was backward-looking rather than forward-looking.

One particularly aggressive approach was being made by Lehman Brothers. It had recently bought Abraham and Company, a relatively small boutique brokerage house, and the integration between the two companies was not going well. Lehman was actively looking for a candidate who could solve the problem and help the company succeed in the institutional brokerage business. I had proved I could do it at

Hutton, something a lot of people in the industry considered impossible. So why not at Lehman?

Lehman's CEO at the time, Pete Peterson, called me and said I needed to come to work there. The former CEO of the Bell & Howell Corporation, Pete had also been the secretary of commerce under President Nixon. He told me that the firm was in great shape, having recovered from its fixed-income debacle in 1972, when it came close to going out of business. Pete was brought in, and with the help of George Ball—the former undersecretary of state in the Kennedy and Johnson administrations (not the same George Ball who became the president of E. F. Hutton)—and with financing from two Italian banks, he was able to right the ship.

Being invited to join Lehman Brothers was flattering, given its long and illustrious history. There was truly a mystique surrounding the prestigious company that only a few firms could claim. In early 1977, Lehman offered me what on the surface looked like an offer that was too good to turn down. After four months of back-and-forth, it agreed to make me president of Lehman Securities, which encompassed institutional, retail (a small but aggressive group), and international businesses. The latter segment was very small, almost nonexistent, but it was very interesting to me, given Lehman's history.

Lehman also offered me a seat on the board, which I believe made me, at age forty-one, the youngest board member in the company's 130-year history. In addition, the package included a relatively large ownership in the firm and a generous boost in salary. But most important, at least to me, was the fact that it was building a massive new trading floor. Lehman assured me that it agreed with my prediction that in the future, trading—and research—would be needed to support investment banking, one of its most important activities.

There was only one thing that gave me pause: my colleagues in the industry had extremely negative things to say about the company. What I kept hearing most often was, "The politics at First Boston and Morgan Stanley are like intermission at Lehman Brothers." But I couldn't imagine anything could be that bad, and besides, I was confident in my own ability to weather the storms.

To me, this job seemed like the next logical step in my career, though the appeal of this new trading floor was really what motivated my decision to join Lehman. It was a snowy night in January of 1977 when I first visited the firm's recently acquired space—four floors at 55 Water Street. On the fortieth floor, it was building one of the largest trading floors in the business.

Lew Glucksman, then the head of trading, walked me around the expansive and impressive forty-thousand-square-foot space and showed me where each of the trading areas was to be located. We walked and talked for a few minutes, then Lew stopped. He paused and pointed to his left.

"This half of the room will be equity, and it will be yours," he said. "The other half will be debt, or fixed income, and it will be mine. We will be partners."

Famous last words. As it would turn out, I never did get half the room. I realized thereafter that there is a big difference between *selling* and *installing*, two things one ought never to confuse.

At Hutton, we employed between ten and twelve traders and thirty analysts. At Lehman, I was going to have as many as fifty or even one hundred analysts and between four hundred and five hundred fixed-income and equity traders on the floor! It was a new approach that seemed liked a natural next step, exactly what I was trying to show my partners at Hutton was the future as I envisioned it.

During our negotiations, Lehman did everything I asked it to do. Much to my surprise, Lew Glucksman and David Sachs, the company's chief legal counsel, even honored my request for them to have dinner at my house with their wives, an invitation I purposely extended as a test. I wanted to see if all the bad things people said about the company and its leadership were actually true. They certainly fooled me that night, because it was a rather pleasant evening.

Afterward, Lew told people it was the first and last time he would ever accept such an invitation. Apparently, he and David had never gone to a business dinner with their wives. That should have tipped me off right there and then, but it didn't.

Even so, and in spite of everything I had heard about Lehman, I still found myself drawn to the company. I have always been an outsider, and I loved troubled business situations that I thought I could fix. Besides, I had a lot of confidence in Pete Peterson. I could easily see where the firm was headed and wanted to be a part of that growth.

Also, I firmly believed that making the transition from managing institutional brokerage exclusively, to managing retail and international brokerage as well, seemed like a good challenge. Abraham and Company wasn't a fit, so this was a chance for me to do what I thought I did best—fix what was broken.

Even though I was cautioned by almost everybody in the industry that my decision to go to Lehman was a real mistake, that it was an impossible place to work, and that my new partner, Lew Glucksman, was a near tyrant, I thought the company was headed in the right direction. And it had made me an offer I simply could not refuse.

I OFFICIALLY LEFT HUTTON in February of 1977, but not before Fomon attempted to make me an almost better offer. However, it was too little too late. Besides, I had already committed to Lehman. When my decision was publicly announced, it prompted a major article in *Institutional Investor* magazine. I was not pleased with the fanfare or exposure: someone once told me that too much PR comes right before jail, especially on Wall Street.

After arriving at Lehman, I was cautioned by a wily old arbitrager, Bernie Latterman, that I had just three months—at the most—to do what I wanted to do before they, especially Lew, would get in my way.

I wasn't sure how to take his warning, but I never forgot it.

I think it's fair to say that when I arrived, Lehman's brokerage business was a mess. The Abraham people felt they had made a mistake in selling, just as Lehman felt they had erred in making the acquisition.

The Lehman group in place before the acquisition was unnecessarily hostile to the Abraham people. To get them together was like trying to negotiate peace in the Middle East.

We were initially housed on a dreary lower floor of Lehman's not-so-quaint offices at 140 Broadway. At the time, the trading floor wasn't even located in the same building as the banking division. This changed shortly after I arrived, when we moved to 55 Water Street.

My new office was actually two corner offices—one that looked up the East River from the fortieth floor and another that overlooked the Statue of Liberty and the Verrazano Bridge from the forty-first floor.

In my mind, these were the ultimate New York City offices. Other perks included the Lehman dining room, which was known as one of the best on Wall Street. Not only was the food top-notch, you also never knew whom you might see there—everyone from the king of Spain to the head of the Federal Reserve.

I quickly learned that there was a great divide between traders and bankers. Bankers viewed traders as inferior, only able to think in the short term. Bankers, on the other hand, were often elitist, blue-blooded, Ivy League–educated, well-connected movers and shakers. I had hoped that this perception would change—and quickly, too. At least that was the pitch that Lehman made to me during the hiring process.

Being a partner at Lehman Brothers was certainly the pinnacle of my career up to that point, but my enjoyment of it would be rather short-lived. It only took me six months to realize I had walked into a hornet's nest. Even with all the warnings, I didn't realize I was going to a place with so many very difficult people.

To make matters worse, many of my former colleagues from Hutton, who I thought would follow me over to Lehman, said, "We love you, Ed, but we won't go to Lehman, even for you." The analysts simply did not believe Lehman was committed to research.

Still, through the art of persuasion and some ninja salesmanship, I got a few analysts, a couple of traders, and some salesmen to come on board. Luckily, Mike Sherman was one of them, and we continued our pas de deux as strategists. Ultimately, with some additional hiring, I got Lehman, which had never been on the all-star list, to around fifteenth place, which put us in business.

LEHMAN SECURITIES SUDDENLY and quite unexpectedly became a nice little business and a significant profit center. I completely revamped the non–New York office management, which turned around the profitability of our regional offices. I hired Steve Spiegel to head up the Chicago office, and this sent a message that, since he was the best manager in that city, we were in the game and should be taken seriously. Almost immediately, we started to increase our market share. We opened an office in London, which helped brokerage flow,[4] and our aggressive retail group helped make the business quite profitable.

This was the beginning of what I have often referred to as a three-year war between Lew Glucksman and me. Although Pete Peterson recruited me, he left Lew and me to fight it out once I was hired.

Pete taught me many things, one being that no matter who you are or where you come from, you need to network. Whenever I watched him at meetings and social events, he always sought out and talked to the smartest or most influential person in the room. That was never important to me, but it should have been. It would have helped other people know who I was and what I was doing. But because of my innate shyness, working a room always made me uncomfortable. This would prove to be a weakness time and time again, one I've never really gotten over. (In the end, you have to *be yourself* and know that's good enough.) From my very first day at Lehman, I attempted to be friends with Lew. When we first started working together, I wanted to believe that he sort of liked me. After all, he was partially responsible for bringing me into the firm. And yet a collegial relationship never came to pass. I am not sure he really liked *anyone*. If he did, he had an awkward way of showing it.

Lew was very astute in many ways and knew more about commercial paper—a kind of short-term debt instrument issued by corporations—than anyone. But he seemed obsessed with power. He did all

---

[4] "Brokerage flow" is simply a trader's term for orders. For example, the stock market in London opens before the one in New York does, and if Lehman's brokers in London could get orders from their clients, then when Lehman opened in New York five or six hours later, the US traders would have merchandise to offer their clients—and more orders would result.

sorts of things to make sure everyone knew *he* was in charge, despite the fact he and Pete both shared the responsibility of running the company and had the titles to go with it.

For example, Lew went out of his way to try to tell me which analysts should write what reports on which banking clients—an absurd assertion coming from him at the time, because managing the analysts was undoubtedly outside his purview.

One thing is certain: it became clear shortly after I arrived that Lew didn't want me there at all. He might have felt threatened by what I was doing with the newly formed institutional side of our partnership. Or he might have felt a duty to live up to his ornery reputation, which everyone warned me about. Or maybe he just enjoyed being feared. Whatever the reason, I was persona non grata almost from day one.

One day quite early in my tenure there, while I was still the newest member of the good old boys' club at Lehman, Lew called me into his office and scolded me! He said I wasn't being a good partner because I wasn't eating lunch often enough in the executive dining room with the others. I carefully explained that I had other things to do during lunch: I was spending my time with my team and talking to clients, busy convincing them that Lehman Brothers wasn't a bad place to do business—that with my presence, things were different now. This logic fell on deaf ears.

The truth is, yes, Lew was partly right. It's important to see and be seen, to let your colleagues know you're united with them and not out to show them up. After a while I did spend more time in the executive dining room, and it turned out to be a pleasant and worthwhile experience.

Everyone in the industry knew Lew was impulsive. He fired people on a whim (including one partner who had a flock of kids), telling them to leave the trading floor for no apparent reason. This impulsive behavior, which became known throughout the industry, made it harder than it should have been for me to hire quality people.

One day, after he had lost a particularly large amount of money on commercial paper trades, he called me up and told me he had just fired four people. He said he wanted me to fire four more! "Bring them to my office," he said.

I arrived a short while later—alone. "Where are your people?" he asked.

I told him he was looking at them: me.

If he was going to fire anyone from my division that day, it was going to be Ed Hajim. Needless to say, I kept my job for the time being, and so did everyone else on my team.

IN 1978, LEHMAN BROTHERS merged with the investment bank Kuhn, Loeb & Company, and the firm thereafter became known as Lehman Brothers Kuhn Loeb. This event has been written about extensively, both in books and academic journals, and I refer you to them if you want to explore some of the details and history behind the merger.

One of the best accounts of the infighting at Lehman in the 1970s and 1980s is *Greed and Glory on Wall Street: The Fall of the House of Lehman*, by the journalist Ken Auletta. It paints what I consider to be an accurate portrait of Lew Glucksman. I'm mentioned in the book several times— including in one passage that says, "Glucksman hated Hajim." I didn't need to read that in a book.

It was not long after the merger that Lew tried to push me out of the company altogether. In his mind, it seemed that the merger had created what is euphemistically called redundancies—multiple people doing the same job within an organization. Usually when that happens, the people considered redundant are going to get fired. At the time, I was head of the brokerage business, and of course there was someone at Kuhn Loeb who was the head of its brokerage business. One of us would have to go.

During my Thanksgiving vacation in 1978, Lew tried to give my job to my Kuhn Loeb counterpart. When I came back and found out that he had tried to pull the rug out from under me, I was livid. I made it clear to Lew that I was more qualified than the guy he was trying to replace me with. In the end, though, the Kuhn Loeb guy was fired, and I kept my position. But Lew told me the reason: "I got along less well with him than I do with you. So you're the man."

———————————

BY THIS POINT, we all knew that Lew was a gruff man, a loner with an erratic, short fuse. You never knew where or when he would explode, but you could count on it. He was also notorious for throwing things, especially his shoes.

Although Lew was a bully prone to temper tantrums, it seemed that people worked harder for him because of his tyrannical behavior. Needless to say, I never agreed with his tactics. I will concede that I learned a lot from him during my time at Lehman, mostly what I *didn't* want to do as a leader. He held up a mirror to me in many ways—showing me the ugly side of what anger in the office looks like and why it doesn't work.

I have to admit that we shared some similarities back then, our unpredictable tempers among them. As I've mentioned, I carried a lot of anger from my childhood, and I'd be lying if I said it didn't spill over into my adulthood. I even threw a phone in the office on a couple of occasions. Barbara will tell you about the time we went on a trip and I forgot my belt: it sent me into a frenzy of rage. And I still get upset when I have a bad game of golf. I understand how easy it is to lose control when you have a reservoir of anger inside you.

I probably inherited this trait from my father. But unlike him, and unlike Lew, I never took out my anger on *anyone else*. My target was always myself.

After watching Lew, I fully understood why that behavior isn't appealing or effective. I never wanted to lead out of fear. I wanted to be someone who inspires, who motivates, who talks the talk *and* walks the walk. I wanted people to know that my goal was for them to be better than even *they* thought they could be—my mantra to this day.

POWER, GREED AND GLORY ON WALL STREET

THE FALL OF LEHMAN BROTHERS

FOR YEARS THE RESENTMENT HAD BEEN BUILDING. And now, at lunch, it began to erupt. Lewis Glucksman, the co-chief executive officer of Lehman Brothers Kuhn Loeb, a short, rumpled man with the face of a Russian general, who was disparaged by Wall Street blue bloods as a lowly "trader," Lew Glucksman would leave the lunch table determined to remove Peter G. Peterson, his imperious co-C.E.O. at the venerable investment banking house, from his job.

BY KEN AULETTA

CHAPTER THIRTEEN

Greed and Glory

c: 1980–1984

THOUGH WE CONSTANTLY BATTLED, Lew Glucksman somehow managed to hold the upper hand. Eventually, he wanted control of Lehman's equities business, meaning the whole trading floor—including my half of it. And like a hungry bird of prey, he waited for just the right moment to strike.

The Kuhn Loeb acquisition brought with it a money-management group that was merged into ours. Both groups were losing assets, and there were complaints about the division management not having the required experience. Lew saw this as an opening, a way to get me out of the room by suddenly pressing me to take over the money management division, called Lemco, short for "Lehman Management Company." Its assets had dwindled from more than $3 billion to just under $2 billion in a short period of time.

It had four funds, including Lehman Corporation, a New York Stock Exchange–listed closed fund. Lemco was almost a separate operation, with very little interface with other parts of the firm.

Lew pushed out Lemco's manager and convinced everyone that I had to take the job because I was the only partner who had previously worked in a money-management company. Plus, I had been president of a mutual fund.

At first, I resisted the change in regime, but I was urged by everyone I trusted to take it on. They said it was something I could sink my teeth into, that it would be my show, with little to no interference or supervision—my preferred modus operandi. I was also able to extract a car and driver out of the company as part of my deal, making my commute to and from Connecticut much easier. At the time, I was told that only Pete and Lew had cars, but the company agreed to give me one—on the sly.

In 1980, I became chairman and CEO of Lemco. I went right to work separating the Lemco business into five profit centers with different leaders and organizational structures. I placed more focus on marketing and client service, which was sorely lacking. I also added a profit center for corporate cash management and put a woman in charge, Theresa Havell, making her, I believe, the first female officer in Lemco's history. We also launched a couple of money market funds, which were essential in those days for a money-management company. The latter caused a war with Lew, because he thought it conflicted with his commercial paper operation. Somehow, though I don't believe anyone thought it would happen, I won that battle.

ONE OF MY FAVORITE PARTNERS AT LEHMAN was Arthur Fried, who was the CFO. One day early on during my tenure at Lemco, he came to my office with a frown on his face and a mission to accomplish. He explained that although I had a lot of talent, I was missing one crucial tool—attention to financial details. At first, I adamantly disagreed with his assessment. After thinking about it for a while, I realized that my main focus *was* on other things—on culture, strategy, and people. The financials usually took care of themselves. At least, that's how things had been up to that point in my career.

Once I admitted this weakness to myself and then to Arthur, he introduced me to a six-foot-five-inch Dartmouth graduate named Steve Blecher. As Arthur assured me, Steve would pay careful attention to all these details and keep me out of trouble. He had done it all in the back office—accounting, IT, HR, legal, you name it. Numbers were in his blood, because his father had done a similar job at Neuberger Berman. Arthur was right: I needed a partner.

Coming to this realization was a true breakthrough for me, because I suddenly recognized that no man can do it all by himself—a lesson I should have learned earlier, at Greenwich Management. Although I had always tried to surround myself with bright, committed people, this was the first time I understood that one of the secrets to success is to find very smart people who do things you can't do, or don't want to do, and to surround yourself with them. It took less than a week for me to realize that Steve was a godsend—and he remained a godsend for the next thirty years.

With Steve on board, I could focus on what I loved—building businesses—and the company soared. We added around forty or fifty new clients in the first two years and lost almost none. Our mutual funds did very well, with the performance of Buzz Zaino's Lehman Capital fund leading the way. Both Bob Buckles, the Lehman Corporation portfolio manager, and Charlie Hetzel, the One William Street fund portfolio manager, turned in excellent numbers, as did the team focused on Taft-Hartley pension plans. These changes and the growth in assets helped Lemco achieve record profits.

We did have a break in mid-1982 as the market bottomed: the team and I got bullish and did some great buying for our funds and clients, which resulted in our having a very good year. Meanwhile, I looked on with amusement when in the midst of this downturn, Lew tried to economize by not serving strawberries in the executive dining room and limiting the number of cigars each partner was allotted at lunch.

AROUND THE MIDDLE OF 1983, the unstoppable Lew started showing signs that he wanted to take over the firm from Pete Peterson.

He had already become co-CEO, but he wanted Pete *out*. Since I was on the board of directors, he wanted my support and vote in this effort. I told him that Pete was not just important to the firm—he was vital to it. With Pete as our "super banker" and Lew running the firm, in my mind, there was no reason to change things. However, my position didn't sit very well with Lew, though I didn't realize at the time how much it annoyed him.

A few weeks passed before I was called into a meeting with Lew and Pete I'll never forget. I thought they were going to put me on the executive committee because of the increasing importance of Lemco. Instead I was told that I was to leave Lemco and join a newly-formed investment banking group. The excuse I was given was that my talents were needed in a more important part of the firm.

Obviously, I vigorously objected to their request. I did my best to stand my ground. I thought it would be hard to remove me because I was the chairman of six mutual funds with outside boards of directors. I was also the chairman of Lehman Corporation, which had its own outside board of directors. Even so, Lew was relentless.

Here is Ken Auletta's account of what happened, from *Greed and Glory on Wall Street*:

> Glucksman transferred Edmund A. Hajim, chairman and CEO of the Lehman Management Company (Lemco), to the banking department. When Hajim went to Peterson to protest, the chairman says he was stunned. How could Lew remove Hajim? Since Hajim had assumed command of the division in 1980, the assets Lemco managed had climbed from $2 billion to more than $10 billion. Though Glucksman himself had recruited Hajim from E. F. Hutton, Glucksman now told Hajim he wanted firmer management of Lemco.

To be blunt, I did not receive much support from my colleagues, either, which took me by surprise. I thought I had some friends in the company.

Even Pete, someone I knew was an ally, told me that Lew's decision was final. Others I approached, including Bob Rubin and Harvey Krueger, were privately sympathetic but could not help. I even went back to Lew and told him I thought I could sell Lemco for between $100 and $200 million, which would give him more capital to trade.

He rejected the idea, and I had no choice but to acquiesce. I moved from Lemco to the new group in July of 1983.

Once I had been moved into banking, I was working *under* Roger Altman (who had previously been the assistant secretary for domestic finance at the US Treasury Department), which meant I had essentially been stripped of all my responsibilities. I had gone from independently managing six divisions and two hundred people with almost $10 billion in assets to having no portfolio and little independence. I had grown one of the most profitable divisions of the firm by 500 percent in less than three years. I had taken on one of the toughest assignments of my career and flourished. But none of that seemed to make a difference. This was personal. Lew was out to get me. In fact, he would later say that this was his reason for moving me—I had grown the business *too* fast.

In *Greed and Glory on Wall Street*, Peter Solomon, one of the firm's managing directors, was quoted as saying the move was "wacko." It did seem irrational, against everything I stood for. But for Lew, the politics and power struggle within the company were more important than anything else. Another lesson learned.

Lew then made his move to push Pete Peterson out of the company. He consummated that unforgettable takeover at our board meeting in October, when Pete was officially asked to leave. At that point, I knew it was time for me to leave as well.

After discussing my angst and discomfort with Barbara, who wanted me to leave much earlier (I never make a big decision without her), I decided to leave Lehman.

This was one of the toughest decisions I ever made.

I had three kids in private school and a large home in Greenwich, and I hadn't made enough money to throw my hands up and say, "Oh, what the hell—it's just a job."

I grew up with a clear understanding that the harder you fall, the more important it is to get right back up and try again. *Falling does not equal failing.* As the late, great baseball legend Yogi Berra once said, "Whenever you come to a fork in the road, take it."

I was at a big fork, and I had to make sure the path I took next would bring me closer to what I wanted to do and give me the freedom to do it. In the past, this meant choosing a job that had the potential for growth and carried a lot of responsibility and authority versus a job that may have paid a higher salary. From early in life, I had always taken the path that moved me in the direction I instinctively wanted to go.

Not surprisingly, I wasn't the only one who decided the time had come to leave the firm. One of the New York newspapers ran a cartoon depicting a number of us jumping off a sinking ship with the name painted on the side: *Lehman*.

THE STREET MUST HAVE BEEN WATCHING what was happening at Lehman, because I was getting a number of interesting calls from many of our competitors. It was just one more example of how lucky I've been throughout my career: as one situation fades or changes, another opportunity usually appears on the horizon.

Several large firms wanted to take a look at me, but I knew that going to another large firm wasn't the answer. I needed to do my own thing. Freedom was calling my name louder than ever before. I had always wanted to be the boss. And having survived the battlefield of Lehman, I had an arsenal of information to take with me. I knew in my gut I wanted to lead my next venture.

I'd been a president, CEO, or chairman ever since I started Greenwich Management in 1969. I liked being in charge, and I thought I was pretty good at it. When you're the boss, it's much easier to give credit away, which I much prefer doing, as opposed to taking it. Besides, although I will accept advice, I've never been very good at being *told* what to do. I need to come to my own conclusions.

In addition to big firms, I had been pursued by Roy Furman and Bernard Selz of Furman Selz Mager Dietz & Birney. Furman Selz was an employee-owned research-driven boutique investment bank founded in 1973, when Bernard Selz and Roy Furman took it over from Mel Seiden. It had offices on three floors at 110 Wall Street and seventy or so employees, including five analysts and three traders.

Furman Selz intrigued me. It was very small but had been in business for ten years and had around $20 million in revenues—tiny compared to Lehman and Lemco. Bernard and Roy had asked me a number of times to come into the firm, and finally the time seemed right. It started off as a casual conversation, but when my former head trader from Hutton, Billy Mattison (who was then at Furman Selz), joined in, I felt excited about the possibilities. I really thought this could be the situation I had always been looking for and working toward.

Furman Selz had one of the most important things I was looking for in a company: a platform. As I learned from my experience at Greenwich Management, it's best to start with an existing business, not from scratch. In addition, Bernard and Roy were eager to have me come on board because they had no interest in running a firm themselves. Bernard wanted to manage money, and Roy wanted to handle the banking business. We structured a deal in which I became the chairman and would be responsible for running all operations of the firm. It was a perfect situation for everyone.

Knowing that Bernard and Roy could not compete with the kinds of offers I was contemplating from larger companies, I suggested eschewing a set salary. Instead, I asked them to give me two-thirds of their own average combined compensation for the first two years, thus tying their performance to mine. The better they did, the better I did.

I also bought stock in the firm, though I owned slightly less than Roy and Bernard did. This was important to me, because my father had taught me the value of ownership from a very early age. "If you're going to be involved with something," he would say, "try to own a piece of it."

WHEN THE TIME CAME TO GIVE MY NOTICE at Lehman, I went directly to Lew and told him I was leaving. I imagine he was delighted. For sure, he was not surprised. But I think he was relieved that I did not go to a competitor. Anyway, I sold back my stock and made about four times my initial investment over the course of seven years.

In 1984, seven months after my departure, as many of us feared but a lot sooner than many of us had expected, Lew took down the firm, again by taking large losses in his commercial paper operation. Forced by his partners, he sold it to Shearson/American Express in a fire sale. The price was probably only slightly more than what I could probably have sold Lemco for a mere year earlier.

This was almost exactly what happened in 1972, when Lew got Lehman involved in the trading of hundreds of millions of dollars' worth—maybe billions of dollars' worth—of commercial paper. This trading activity was highly leveraged, and Lehman lost a great deal of money. Afterward, as I mentioned, Pete Peterson had to get financing from two Italian banks to save the firm. (All this is well documented not only in *Greed and Glory on Wall Street* but also in Stephen Schwarzman's book, *What It Takes*.)

It was a sad ending to a once fine and glorious 135-year-old lady whose history I am proud to have been part of, if only for a short period.

With Corey and Brad, in front of the pyramids, Egypt (1992)

CHAPTER FOURTEEN

Egypt, the Galapagos Islands, India, and Beyond!

BEFORE WE HAD CHILDREN, Barbara and I read several books about child development written by noted psychologists. According to them, spending time with your children is important, but spending *quality* time with them is even more key. I subscribed to this notion and tried to make the time we spent together focused and fun.

Barbara and I had agreed early on in our marriage that we would have a division of labor. I would be the "hunter-gatherer," while she would be in charge of the home and family. Nevertheless, I still tried to be an attentive and involved dad. And for the most part, I think I succeeded. G. B. and Brad attended the Brunswick School, a private boys' school in Greenwich, and Corey attended Greenwich Academy, a private school for girls. (In the eighth grade, she transferred to the Greenwich Country Day School, and in tenth grade, to the Middlesex School, a boarding school in Concord, Massachusetts.) Despite my busy schedule, I was able to participate in the kids' activities: I went to their plays and poetry readings and to their athletic events, and I tried to be home for dinner almost every night.

One of the things that cemented us together as a family was our vacations, which we took together on a regular basis. First, there was the famous road trip across Canada when we moved back East from

California. It initiated a love of travel that has continued to this day. Whether we travel only with each other or with our children and/or grandchildren, we're always up for a trip and energized by it!

Toward the beginning of our marriage, we had a getaway trip all arranged to Mexico and had hired a babysitter to take care of G. B. When the sitter canceled, we just decided to take him with us and discovered that it was easier than we thought to travel with a two-year-old. After that, we traveled often with G. B. and continued the tradition with all the kids. For example, G. B. joined us on a memorable ski trip to Aspen, where Barbara skied for the very first time. She fell in love with the beautiful snowy slopes of Colorado, and it was so much fun to have the baby along. The addition of two more children didn't deter us from travel.

I clearly remember Corey blowing out her first birthday candle at the lodge in Sugarbush, Vermont. The children learned to ski on the trails of the Okemo Mountain Resort, also in Vermont, where we rented the basement of a ski house comprising one bedroom and one bath. For some crazy reason, we took our cat and dog along on the trip with us. And hilariously, we all barely fit in the small quarters. After that, skiing during the Christmas break became a family tradition.

However, skiing in New England had its drawbacks: either the temperature was below freezing or it was so warm that all we saw was rain and mud. One winter, Barbara, who loved sunshine, came up with the idea to change the venue and charter a forty-foot trimaran in the British Virgin Islands. The trip was such a huge success that we gave up skiing during the Christmas break and made our boat vacation an annual excursion. It was incredible. We snorkeled and water-skied while G. B. and Brad learned to scuba dive. When the children got older, we chose a book for all of us to read and discuss, the first being *Who Moved My Cheese? An Amazing Way to Deal with Change in Your Work and in Your Life*, by Dr. Spencer Johnson.

Our later trips included some of the kids' friends: Kate and Bart Osman, Charles Baillie, and Jamie Claar, as well as Jim and Marthe, who would become, respectively, our son-in-law and daughter-in-law.

I think we would unanimously vote these trips as our favorite times together, hands down.

While skiing continued to be a part of our family travel, instead of going to Vermont over the Christmas vacation, we chose the March break to visit ski resorts in Utah, Wyoming, Idaho, and Colorado. We fell in love with Vail, where we ended up buying a condo.

Summer camp also played a big part in our children's lives. At age eight, each of them left for New Hampshire, where they spent eight glorious weeks. That was a pretty nice vacation for Barbara and me as well!

Each summer Barbara and I would take a trip to Europe, where we rented a car and toured various countries. There are too many stories and not enough pages in this book to tell all these tales. But I think these trips kept our marriage fresh and offered us a great break from everyday life. Then, after camp was over and before school started, we would take a family trip to various locales, including Bermuda, with Barbara's mom and dad, and Sea Pines, in South Carolina.

On the professional side of things, my participation in YPO (Young Presidents' Organization), a global leadership community of chief executives, was also an important part of my life. Some of the highlights were trips to Hong Kong, Shanghai, Cape Town, and Thailand. We also took our children to the YPO family universities in Bermuda, Colorado, and Sweden.

Barbara and I became very good friends with a Harvard Business School classmate of mine, Charlie Baillie, and his wife, Marilyn. Charlie eventually became the chairman and CEO of the Toronto-Dominion Bank. But back then they lived in New York City and loved to travel even more than we did. One weekend evening, after a few glasses of wine, we concocted the idea that we should take our two families to Africa. The Baillies had four children—Charles, Matt, Jonathan, and Alexandra, who were around the same ages as our kids. The children knew each other a little but weren't close friends. However, we took a leap of faith and planned the trip anyway.

It was an amazing experience, such a success that we subsequently went on trips together every other year to places such as Egypt, the Galapagos Islands, Patagonia, and India! Through the experiences of all these trips, our families have become lifelong friends. (Our second to last trip together took place in 2000, when we went to Scotland for the wedding of Charles and his wife, Suzanne.)

Once the children left home, nothing stopped Barbara and me from traveling. Most of these trips have been taken with our great friends Tom and Mary Alice O'Malley. Tom is known as one of the most prominent CEOs in the oil refining business. I served on one of his boards for ten years. Tom was also the former chairman of Manhattan College's board of trustees and provided the largest gift in Manhattan College history. On the road together, our all-time favorite place to visit was Ascona, Switzerland. Luckily, Tom and Mary Alice speak German, because it's a place that has remained undiscovered by Americans.

Our home life wasn't all about vacations and travel. Parties were also a big part of what we did! And we loved giving them, most notably our Christmas Spirits party and Opera Cup brunch.

At Christmastime during our Connecticut years, we invited all our friends, and eventually our adult children's friends, to the house for a great buffet and hot buttered rum. It was quite the tradition and missed by our friends when we left Greenwich. We continued that tradition in Nantucket after we built our home there. But instead of a holiday dinner, we began hosting a brunch the morning of a famous Nantucket wooden boat race called the Opera Cup. We invited people to come over at 10:00 a.m. to watch the race from our home while enjoying a buffet breakfast. Each year our friend Barbara Daly helped Barbara design a mug that we gave to our guests as a party favor. We hoped that someday the mugs might become collector's items. We held this party for twenty-five years! We were begged to continue having it, but enough was enough!

Fortunately, our next-door neighbors on Nantucket, Anne Marie and Doug Bratton, purchased John Kerry and Teresa Heinz's house on the island, two doors from ours. Barbara persuaded them to continue the tradition and take over the party. It continues, mugs and all.

TRIPS AND PARTIES ASIDE, during our time in Greenwich, Barbara worked at the Brunswick School in various capacities for sixteen years, ending up as the director of development. At one point after leaving that job, she was offered the position of head of the lower school, which she decided against taking. She subsequently became one of the trustees, an office she held for nine years, breaking the school's six-year term-limit rule.

My own involvement with the school started as such things usually do—with a small unsolicited donation to the annual fund, which I made when G. B. was in first grade. This was followed by a phone call from a pleasant-voiced woman in the development office, who asked me if I would like to be the class representative for the fund. It would require "no work," because she would make all the solicitation calls. Barbara urged me to get involved, and I foolishly said yes.

Well, after I made twenty or so calls, and after I attended a meeting nearly every month for twelve months, the fund raised a record amount of money (although it would be considered minuscule by today's standards). The result was predictable: five or so years later, I was elected to the board of trustees, and in 1980, I became its chair.

Part of the reason I agreed to do this was that I thought I had a chance to merge Greenwich Academy, an all-girls school, with the Brunswick School, an all-boys school, forming a coeducational institution. I also thought it would be possible to merge Greenwich Country Day School with the other two, thus combining all the schools in Greenwich and creating what could have been one of the top coed private schools in the country.

But a more-than-one-hundred-year-old girls' school did not want to change its tradition. We arrived at a compromise in which Greenwich Academy and Brunswick would integrate classes in grades nine through twelve (e.g., Brunswick would teach physics and Greenwich Academy would teach chemistry), with both boys and girls together in each of the classes.

I was convinced that it was vital for boys and girls to learn to work together. Boys in particular would have to learn that in the professional world they were entering, it was very likely they would have a female boss or supervisor. Fortunately, the coordination program has been very successful, and I believe both schools have benefited from the arrangement. While I was chair, the headmaster was Norm Pedersen, who over his nineteen years as headmaster had transformed Brunswick from just a good school to one of the best in New England. He was followed by one of the most popular teachers, Duncan Edwards, whom Barbara had worked for while she was at Brunswick and who took the school to a whole new level. It is now recognized as one of the finest private schools in the country. Among the many things Edwards did was to supervise the building of an entirely new campus, which bears his name today.

At around the same time, I became a trustee of the American Craft Museum, now called the Museum of Art and Design, in New York City, and was involved in moving the museum into its new quarters on West 53rd Street. A few years later, I was asked to be the board's chair, but I quickly turned down the opportunity, realizing it was too big a commitment of finances and time. One of my colleagues suggested that the position could serve as my "social currency," but I wasn't interested in going to a lot of black-tie dinners, nor did I want to overextend myself, especially when I was going to be starting an important new job at Furman Selz.

FURMAN SELZ TO XEROX

Ed Hajim gets the right come-on.

Furman Selz Chairman Edmund Hajim had been propositioned before, but never quite so persuasively. But it wasn't just the $110 million purchase price that made Xerox's unsolicited offer so seductive, Hajim says. It was the promise of unlimited capital in the future.

And capital for what? Merchant banking, of course (see story page 58). "We've never been able to take large positions in businesses we liked," explains Hajim. "During the 1970s, for instance, we missed opportunities in hospital management and cable TV for lack of available capital. With Xerox behind us, we can take those Merritt, a fixed-income investment banker and mutual fund manager and Crum and Forster, a property and casualty insurance company, can and will provide a ready source of mezzanine financing in future Furman Selz deals.

Founded in 1973, Furman Selz Mager Dietz & Birney is best known for its equity research department. After the sale is final, Hajim and the other nine principals in the firm will remain at their

CHAPTER FIFTEEN

Back in Control

c. 1986–1987

I OFTEN DESCRIBE THE DIFFERENCE between Lehman and Furman Selz this way: at Lehman, when I wanted refreshment, I would pick up the phone at my desk, and shortly thereafter a tuxedo-clad butler would appear in my office carrying a glass of perfectly chilled iced tea. At Furman Selz, a bell would go off in my seat and I would get up and get it myself.

And you know what? I loved it.

Furman Selz wasn't glamorous. There was no fancy dining room on the forty-third floor and no award-winning chef, as there were at Lehman. In fact, the window in my small office looked onto the wall of the building next door. But I didn't care. From my point of view, the important thing was that for the first time in my career, I was making a bet totally on myself. I had been successful in a number of things, and I wanted to prove I could do it again—as a leader. A new kind of freedom had *finally* arrived.

At that point in my career, I'd learned that before taking any new job it was critical to try to understand the differences between the place I was leaving and the place I was going to. I needed to consider all the characteristics of the new company, including its size, reputation, location, and, most of all, its people. I needed to figure out which of my skills would be a good fit in that environment.

I also knew that it would be unwise for me to start making signifi-cant changes until after I'd carefully analyzed the situation and built a plan in writing. I knew that as soon as a new person enters an organi-zation, that organization inevitably changes.

Think of it like this: when a foreign body enters any system, that system instantly responds, sometimes in unpredictable, even undesir-able, ways. If I were to do too much too soon, it might have negative consequences. I needed to be strategic and analyze what needed to be fixed and how. My entry had to be done carefully and methodically, and I needed to make a plan before I started to make changes.

At Furman Selz, I began by interviewing all the employees and devising plans for all parts of the business. I took notes on what each department did; I gathered background information on its clients, its strategy, and the determinants of its success. The process took nearly ninety days to complete, but it was time well spent.

Then I hired Steve Blecher, my former partner at Lehman, to be the COO and run the back-office operations. The reaction from Roy and Bernard was, "We thought you were going to do all that!" But I made it clear that Steve and I performed different functions and that his pres-ence was absolutely necessary. (Years later, Bernard told me that Steve was the best hire they ever made.)

Next, I relocated the firm uptown, to 230 Park Avenue, because most of our clients were located in midtown, and the clients who came in from out of town would stay at midtown hotels. All they had to do now was walk out of their hotels and into our offices. Not to mention that all our employees' commutes were going to be shorter.

We also started hiring new people in addition to Steve. Roy found a young lawyer, Brian Friedman from Wachtell, Lipton, Rosen & Katz, who not only had an MBA and an LLD but was also a CPA. Even though he was just twenty-nine years old, he had already done a num-ber of banking deals. He was exactly what our division needed. Next I hired a new head of the prime brokerage business, Mike Petrycki, who was a friend of Steve's. I also hired a head of international sales, Roger Felberbaum, a man I poached from Lehman in order to grow the international brokerage business. We continued to add a number of analysts, salesmen, and traders to improve our position as an institutional broker.

I also formed an executive committee that consisted of Roy, Bernard, and me, which met every Monday at 4:00 p.m. without fail. Further, I mandated that our board of directors (comprising all division heads as well as a few other important people) would meet monthly.

At the weekly meetings, I made sure everything we were doing was well known to Roy and Bernard. After the first few months, things must have been going better than they expected, because they left me pretty much alone, just the way I like it. They went on to do what they loved. Bernard compiled one of the best long-term records in the money-management business and was a major contributor to the firm's profits. Roy hired Michael Garin, and the two of them built one of most successful media and entertainment businesses on Wall Street. The board meetings were a lot like Quaker meetings, because the division heads got a chance to speak and give a report about their divisions or groups. After each person had presented the month's activities—and the month's numbers—we figured out how we could help one another. Still, though it was a fresh start, there were a few rough edges to soften. Why? Because there were still some longtime board members who predated my hiring. And they wanted to keep things the same as they always had been. They did not like many of the changes I was making.

Camilla Dietz, one of the original partners, headed foreign sales. In addition, she served as an analyst on a number of industries, did some banking, and I believe managed some money. She was pretty good at all the jobs, but that way of doing things didn't fit my idea of the best way to grow the firm. I wanted people focused on their real passions and competencies. So I asked her to pick one or two jobs and concentrate on them exclusively. She did that and excelled, as did Ezra Mager, who focused on banking.

But Jim Birney, who was a superb analyst, did not like what I was doing or how I was doing it. He disagreed with the changes I was making, and he finally left the firm at the end of 1986. Even though the firm had more than doubled in size, he was unhappy and a bit disgruntled when he left. His departing words to me were, "Your plan will result in the firm drowning in red ink."

I was sorry to lose Jim, but change was necessary.

I took responsibility for compensation and promotion away from the board and gave it to the executive committee, which greatly reduced conflict. Before I arrived, the year-end bonuses for every employee, from the mail clerks to the founding partners, was decided on by the board. In 1983, during my first year, I watched board discussions grow so heated that they ended with people angrily walking out of meetings without a satisfactory resolution. That's why I put an end to these debates and put the power in the hands of the division heads and the executive committee. Nobody knew what the bonuses were except the three of us and Steve Blecher.

We progressed very well, with record years in '84 and '85, and we began to establish ourselves as competitive in a number of businesses. By 1986, revenues were at $75 million, up from just $20 million in 1983.

THE YEAR 1986 turned out to be a tough one, and some at Furman Selz questioned my strategy. This was the year Jim Birney left, but it was also the year I started the practice of selling between 5 and 10 percent of the firm to our employees each year. The purpose of this was to give employees a chance to participate in the profits and reallocate ownership in a way that favored those who actually produced the profits. We sold these shares at book value, a practice that became part of the compensation structure.

At the end of 1986, I had a little trouble selling stock and only sold a minimal amount because the outlook was somewhat cloudy. Bonuses weren't very big, so many employees were questioning whether the firm's stock was a good investment.

At the time, our industry was going through a period of consolidation. Big firms were buying up small ones. We had no interest in selling

Furman Selz. But in the spring of 1987, one of my old partners from Lehman, George Wiegers, then at Dillon Read, called to ask if I would consider selling the company to Xerox. That kind of sale would be a game changer, so I agreed to speak with him.

Without telling anyone except Steve, I explored the possibility with Mel Howard, the Xerox Financial Services CEO. Their bankers indicated that we would be offered more than *three times* Furman Selz's book value, an offer too attractive to ignore. The more I thought about it, the better and more appealing it became, especially since I was starting to get bearish on the world. (That was an instinctive feeling that came upon me a number of times in my fifty-year run on Wall Street.) I immediately told Roy and Bernard about the offer.

They agreed with me that the deal was intriguing and definitely worth pursuing.

I found out during the discussions with Xerox that a consulting firm had recommended to Xerox that it get into the financial services business. Why? At the time, Xerox sold its machines to its customers on credit in the following way: instead of buying the machines outright, purchasers borrowed the money from Xerox and repaid it in installments, as a loan. Xerox already had a credit infrastructure in place.

The consultants figured that someday the business-machine market was going to level off, and because Xerox was already in the credit business, why not expand and move into financial services to hedge against a future downturn?

Executives at Xerox took the advice and diversified. They bought an insurance company, Crum & Forster, and a fixed-income operation, Van Kampen Merritt. The only other thing they needed was an equity company—and that's where Furman Selz came in.

It was only near the end of the process that I introduced Roy and Bernard to Mel, who was representing Xerox in the negotiations. Xerox had wanted to meet our firm's founders. But in my opinion, this was like all negotiations—the fewer people involved, the better. I was provided with a great example of why this is so at a meeting near the close, when Mel asked if we had any questions.

Bernard—who was willing to voice his opinions and reservations about anything—blurted out, "Why would Xerox want to buy us?"

After I stuttered a bit and before Mel could answer, I cited five good reasons why we were attractive to Xerox and tried to stare down my partner.

Bernard had a point—some directors of Xerox were asking the same question.

Luckily, we moved forward with the deal. A reporter from *Institutional Investor* magazine got wind of it, however, and wanted to talk with us about the negotiations. I made it very clear that no one should talk to him, because if anyone did, the magazine would undoubtedly have publicly asked Bernard's question, and that might have blown the deal.

For us, the deal was a "must do." We needed Xerox's financial resources, and I was going to get it done.

On October 1, 1987, Xerox Financial Services acquired Furman Selz for $110 million (plus a $15 million retention bonus for nonstockholders), which was a lot of money in those days. And at three times the book value, it was a generous assessment—close to the highest valuation ever paid for a brokerage firm.

As luck would have it, we closed just three weeks before the market crash of '87, after which I do not think our firm would even have sold at book value.

Skill is important, but luck is essential.

PART THREE

Bringing Closure

Furman Selz Executive Committee (1993)

CHAPTER SIXTEEN

A Tale of Two Mergers

c. 1987–1993

WHEN WE SOLD FURMAN SELZ TO XEROX, my share of the proceeds amounted to approximately $10 million. For the first time in my life, I had real money. The question became what I should do with it. I had an epiphany: real estate.

When the stock market crashed in 1987, the real estate market crashed with it. Prices were near historic lows, and it seemed like the perfect time to invest. The prospect probably appealed to me so much because, before I met Barbara, I had never had a real home. It seemed like fate.

Before the Furman Selz sale, we had taken a family trip to the Ocean Reef Club in Key Largo, Florida. It was the most idyllic place, a private community featuring golf, tennis, a world-class marina, fine dining, a medical center, and even its own private airport. While we were there with the idea of an investment property in mind, a fast-talking real estate agent persuaded us to buy a 1,200-square-foot condo, complete with a dock, for $105,000.

Great buy. He said he could not only find financing for it but would also find renters for both the dock and the apartment. We would never have to pay anything beyond the $5,000 down payment. It seemed too good to pass up, so Barbara and I bought it, even though we would probably be able to get there only once a year.

Later I found out that the mortgage rate was 13.5 percent! Even so, the agent was right about one thing: we never had to pay anything beyond the down payment. The rental income from the condo and the dock covered all expenses.

With our success in purchasing a home back in 1975, and with the success of the Florida experiment, Barbara and I continued to expand our real estate holdings in 1987. I began to think that it would be wise to buy properties throughout the country where I might someday want to live. And I might not be able to afford to buy them if I waited.

Between 1987 and 1990, we bought land and condos in Vail, Colorado; Scottsdale, Arizona; and Nantucket. We also sold the condo in the Ocean Reef Club and bought a larger one. At the same time, we bought another property, a vacant piece of land in Ocean Reef with water on three sides, that we would not build on until eleven years later.

Our place in Vail was a fifth-floor apartment in the Vail Village Inn, located on the town's main square. It was 2,500 square feet and had a view of the entire valley. The building had gone bankrupt, and because the bank was selling the apartments, the price was very reasonable. Since we all loved to ski, this became a regular vacation spot for the family.

At the time, Barbara's mother, Mae, was living in Scottsdale, in a new development called McCormick Ranch. A few miles north of her home was a development under construction called Desert Mountain, comprising five thousand acres of gorgeous scenery 2,500 feet above sea level. We bought several plots of land there, but we ended up not building on any of them. Even though we enjoyed visiting Mae, neither one of us particularly cared for the desert. We sold those plots a few years later.

In 1986, Barbara and I visited Nantucket, and Barbara immediately fell in love with it. After only a few hours, she said, "Let's find a real estate agent." We did—but we wound up looking for four years! We made frequent bids but kept missing out on properties until October of 1990, when by a stroke of luck a piece of property came on the market that was right on the water at the entrance to the harbor. It was perfect. We subsequently built our dream house—now a cherished family home, a place for our children and grandchildren to gather in the summertime and during holidays.

There were many times over these years when I thought back to my childhood, living with foster families and in orphanages, sleeping in communal bedrooms with no privacy, stuck in places that were hardly beautiful. I thought to myself, for someone who didn't have even *one* home, how did I end up with four of the most beautiful homes in the world, much less in some of the most picturesque locations on the planet? I'm still not sure I know the full answer. It was almost surreal. And I am truly grateful.

———————

AFTER FURMAN SELZ WAS ACQUIRED, I reported to Mel Howard and became a member of the board of Xerox Financial Services. Immediately I was pleased to discover that being part of Xerox completely changed our ability to get things done.

We were subsequently able to borrow money easily to expand our businesses. We were also able to make acquisitions. We bought Shields Asset Management, which had $3.5 billion in assets, for around $22 million, bringing our assets under management up to $12 billion. At about the same time, we were also quite fortunate to acquire Swergold, Chefitz, which was a well-known healthcare investment banking boutique. However, after the crash of 1987, although the market did eventually rebound, it did not usher in a period of great conditions for the world of finance. We had a good '88 and '89, but everyone ran into trouble in '90. Although we did make a small profit, it wasn't big enough to allow for bonuses for our management, which made our deal look a little more legitimate to the Xerox board. But our small profit stood in stark contrast to Kidder Peabody's rumored $300–$400 million loss. This gave bragging rights to David Kearns, Xerox's CEO, when he would chat with

Jack Welch of General Electric, who had bought Kidder Peabody at around the same time Xerox acquired us.

Unfortunately, Xerox's strategy of diversifying into financial services, which was carried out almost entirely by acquisition, started to falter within our first year. It was mostly because of the decline in earnings in Crum & Forster, the insurance company, which was the biggest part of the group. In addition, Xerox's real estate subsidiary required a large infusion of capital, which the board refused to provide. This resulted in the ouster of Mel Howard. It also looked like it would result in the divestiture of the financial businesses.

At the time, we were in the middle of trying to acquire a $7.5 billion asset manager—Seligman Asset Management, twice as large as Shields—for a very reasonable price. This acquisition would have put us in great shape to compete as one of the fastest-growing newcomers in the industry. But with the change in Xerox's strategy, the word went out: no more capital, no more growth. The board began to quietly determine how it could rid itself of these businesses.

The new head of the division, Stu Ross, understood our desire for growth, but he had his marching orders. As a result, we lost the Seligman acquisition. At that point, Steve and I almost left the company. We were going to buy Seligman ourselves, but we didn't know what would happen to our team if we left. We felt responsible for them, so we reluctantly let the opportunity pass. This turned out to be a major financial mistake for both of us, because Seligman was later sold for many hundreds of millions of dollars.

During all this turmoil, my partners at Furman Selz were all over me to make a bid to buy Furman Selz back, but I fought them off, saying Xerox would eventually come to us and then we would be in a much better negotiating position.

Finally, one afternoon in 1992, I got the call I had been waiting for. Xerox was going to sell us to a group headed by Peter Cohen, who later founded Ramius Capital. I knew our bankers didn't want to be part of his firm, and most of our employees didn't want to be sold to *anyone*.

I told the senior management at Xerox that if that happened, many of our people would leave because the noncompete clauses in their contracts had expired. It would not be a wise move. After a few more unsuccessful attempts at a sale, Xerox decided to sell the firm back to us—no big deal for Xerox, because we were the smallest company in the group.

To be fair to Xerox, a few months before we bought Furman Selz back, I sold Shields Asset Management to Dave Williams at BernsteinMcCaulay (part of Alliance Capital) for $80 million and gave Xerox the proceeds. When we bought back the rest of the firm for around $100 million, Xerox actually made money on the purchase—probably the only company to do so during the brokerage firm acquisition binge of the eighties.

When all was said and done, we were independent again, around twice the size we were when Xerox bought us. We flourished while being part of its organization, but we were back on our own.[5]

In order to ensure that the stock distribution was fair, I made a list of the twenty top partners in the firm, set aside 80 percent of the stock, and asked each of them to decide how much they would award themselves and the other nineteen executives. I thought this was a clever way of *not* having to play God. I could observe the varying allotments they determined for their peers and tell those who felt their percentages were too low that I had nothing to do with it. I actually benefited from this strategy because they gave me a disproportionate amount—so in the end, I took some of the stock allocated to me and spread it out to those who I thought deserved a little more than they had received. Complaints were handled simply by saying, "Your partners gave you 2 percent, and I added half a percent from my allocation."

But very few complaints came after my explanation.

I offered the remaining 20 percent of the stock to 180 people, giving them a stake in the company—the total count being two hundred partners! To me, it was important that almost everyone have some ownership in the firm.

---

[5] The full story of the buyback is chronicled in a 2005 Harvard Business School case study, "Furman Selz LLC (A): A Tale of Two Acquisitions" (case number 905–066).

DURING THE TWO DECADES BETWEEN 1973 AND 1993, more than half the country's brokerage firms and investment banks either merged with one another or went out of business. Furman Selz's survival was considered by many to be miraculous.

The only major management change we made after the buyback was to move Brian Friedman, our head of investment banking, who had done an outstanding job of building our banking business, to a new merchant banking division, which was his first love. After a broad search, we brought in one of my former Lehman partners, Bill Shutzer, to manage investment banking. Bill brought with him a great group of clients, including companies such as Tiffany, and a number of young bankers, including Noah Gottdiener, Gerry Cromack, and Rohit Manocha. After the usual bumps in the road that come with management changes, everyone meshed well with Bill. And he took our banking business to the next level. We also added a new director of research, Jim Balog, when Mike Weisberg, our then director of research, who had built a great team, asked to form his own hedge fund and move to the money-management side of the business. Fred Fraenkel also joined us as part of the management of our securities group.

Things went very well for us in '93 and '94, but we started to see problems with a number of our businesses toward the end of '95. We were doing too many things we were not good at, a key mistake in business that should always be avoided. We began divesting and closing down divisions that either didn't align with our strengths or were losing money.

For example, we closed our fixed-income division after it lost around $10 million; and we sold the commercial real estate business for $5 million to Southern Pacific. But the most painful decision of all was selling our mutual fund services business, which John Pileggi had built from scratch with a little help from me. John had done a terrific job, but the industry was consolidating and his business was shrinking. We decided to sell it before it shrank any more to our biggest competitor for $15 million. With all these reductions, we simplified our business and returned to things we did well—investment banking, institutional brokerage, money management, and prime brokerage.

Jan 24, 199[7]

Dear Mrs. Hoffman,

This will obviously come as a shock to you but I believe I am your son, Ed, born on July 26, 1936 in Los Angeles, Calif. For all these years, I believed that you had passed away in childbirth sometime in 1939 as my father had told me. This was not a simple life and when he died in 1971, he left a suitcase which I did not fully go through until late last year. There was enough information there to indicate you did not

Letter to my mother (1997)

The first meeting with Sophie and Phil (1996)

CHAPTER SEVENTEEN

A Suitcase of Letters

c. 1996–1997

BEFORE I GET BACK to tracing the history of my business life, I want to pause and acknowledge the person I rely on more than anyone else—my wife, Barbara.

In my heart, from the time I married Barbara, I knew that I had picked the perfect partner. In 1996, when I turned sixty, I remember looking around our home in Greenwich, and taking an inventory of the incredible life she and I shared with our children. Looking at the family photos of our many adventures, and being surrounded by our children and grandchildren, I just couldn't believe how lucky I was.

Evangelist Billy Graham's wife, Ruth, once wisely wrote, "A happy marriage is a union of two good forgivers." How true that is.

Of course, Barbara and I don't have a perfect relationship—no one does. But we work on it every day because it's totally worth it. When we do have an argument or see things differently, we don't let that bump in the road bother us. In fact, Barbara and I have a rule that we never go to bed angry. By evening time, we forgive, and we quickly forget, which is probably one secret to our enduring marriage.

Many couples today often exercise the option of separation or divorce when a major marital problem comes along. Maybe it's a result of my Catholic school education, but I've always felt that marriage is permanent. You only get married *once*. Sure, people don't stay the same throughout their lives; they're continually changing and evolving. The young person you married is definitely different five, ten, or fifty years later! This means you have to adapt. And in that way, marriage is always a work in progress.

One secret to our marriage is that Barbara and I have never let more than two or three months go by without spending time *alone* together. It's just the two of us. Whether it's a vacation or a weekend or just an evening out for dinner, we forget about everything else going on in our daily lives and relax and appreciate each other. It's the way we tell each other, "You're important to me. And I love you."

Of course, we do have our arguments. But neither one of us has ever stormed out of the house in a fury. We've learned to say, "Forgive me—I'm a little off today." Or we offer an apology or explanation. The rule is never to go to sleep mad at each other.

The truth is that she and I have very little in common! She was raised in a comfortable household with a loving family in a neighborhood she never left until she went to college. I was raised with no parents and no siblings in multiple foster homes and orphanages with no financial resources whatsoever. Obviously, our origins were completely different.

Barbara is outgoing and social, whereas I'm serious and reserved. I was an athlete; she wasn't. She's interested in the arts; I'm interested in the sciences. You get the idea! Barbara, for her part, would not completely agree that we have little in common. We love to dance, she points out, and that is true. We love travel. We both love to play golf. But some of the most important things we *do* have in common are our values and our devotion to hard work and creating a beautiful life for our children and grandchildren. These are the blessings I count every day.

———

BY 1996, I WAS FEELING AS ENERGETIC AS I EVER HAD, and I was totally consumed with work at Furman Selz. The kids were all grown, and we all went about our separate lives. Still, I regularly ruminated about my father and our history together. I made a point of occasionally visiting his grave site in Fort Lauderdale. In fact, I would have gone even more often if I had not been in New York.

As the months passed, 1996 turned out to be a year of unexpected surprises, changes, and healing. It started when Barbara threatened to throw away the suitcase of letters I retrieved from my father's apartment after his death, that had been stashed in our closet for twenty-five years, unopened, since 1971. Not opening it was a kind of denial. I wanted to keep that compartment literally closed, as it might reveal an avenue of pain I didn't want to face.

In my life, I had always wanted to look forward, not backward. It was a kind of defense that had served me well in terms of my business endeavors. But on a personal level, I had things to resolve.

Barbara urged me to go through the suitcase and figure out whether it contained anything worth keeping. If I did not, she was going to throw it out. She was right: memories of my father had hung around long after his death, and the impact of his abandonment on my life had never really gone away. I needed closure. And once and for all, I needed to deal with my feelings. It was definitely time.

As I opened the suitcase, I discovered that my father had kept every single letter I'd ever written! Most of them, filled with childhood and adolescent emotion, had gone unanswered. As I sifted through the handwritten pages, a kaleidoscope of memories rushed back in. I could actually see myself at the time I had written each letter, many of them expressing my innocent need for connection to my father. I could see how desperately I missed him and how confused I often was about why he had been gone for so long. To say the least, it wasn't easy looking through those many years of correspondence. I almost put it all away until I came across a separate bundle of letters I didn't expect to find. These were exchanges between my father and *mother*.

This was the great mystery of my life. What had really happened to my mother? My father had always been so secretive about her and dismissive of my questions. But here, in a startling letter, I discovered that my parents had actually divorced when I was three years old! This meant that my mother *didn't* die in childbirth after he kidnapped me from St. Louis.

I was stunned.

For years, Barbara had an instinctive feeling my mother was still alive. Call it feminine intuition or just a hunch, but to Barbara, there were pieces of my story that simply didn't add up. She had always sensed that my father had held back information about my early years for unexplained reasons.

My curiosity about what happened to my mother became my sole focus. Apprehensive but determined, I hired a private investigation firm to see if it could fill in some of the details about what might have really happened to her. The only information we had was the address of the house where she was last known to be living, my parents' marriage and divorce records, my birth certificate, and her name—Sophie Levin.

For the first few months, the private investigators had difficulty coming up with anything about her, but then they hit a home run using marriage license records. One evening, they called me at home in Greenwich and said that they had found a woman who matched the description I'd given them, though she was by then using the last name of Hoffman.

Wait.

I couldn't believe what I was hearing.

"My mother is still *alive*?" I asked the investigators. That I never expected.

"It appears that she is," they said.

A thousand questions flooded my mind. My heart was beating so hard that I was practically hyperventilating. Barbara could see how shocked I was by the news as she held her hand to my chest.

"Is she okay?" This was the first question that popped out of my mouth.

The investigators told me she was an eighty-one-year-old widow living by herself in an apartment in St. Louis. Her husband had died a few years prior, and at this point in her life, she was quite involved in her local synagogue, living a quiet life.

I turned to Barbara, who could see the look of complete astonishment on my face. I then shared the unbelievable news with her.

"I knew it!" she said. "I just knew she was still alive."

This stunning discovery was a revelation for many reasons. Everything I had believed about my life for nearly sixty years had suddenly been turned upside down. It made me stop cold. My father had told me a horrible lie. And he had perpetuated that lie for my entire life. He knew I had a mother. He knew I needed her. And he had selfishly deprived me of her. I didn't know where to begin in untangling this mess. My anger toward him was renewed in a way that I had never experienced before. How could he have done this? What would have driven him to hurt me this way? I felt I no longer could trust my knowledge of what was the truth and what wasn't.

Above all, I was abruptly and unexpectedly faced with a tough decision—whether I was ready to meet my mother or not. This prospect was kind of frightening. Opening up that suitcase was like opening Pandora's box, a source of great and unexpected surprises. But this box was actually filled with *good* news!

Barbara and I discussed this dilemma for weeks. Was it a good idea for me to reach out to my mother? What were the benefits of inviting this "stranger" into our lives *now*? Why not leave well enough alone? How would this affect our children? Moreover, did we have it in us to nurture this relationship? What if my mother rejected me?

There was certainly a good chance that my mother might be uncomfortable hearing from a long-lost son. Or she might be angry or just uninterested. Perhaps what my father had told me was true—that he had protected me because she never wanted children in the first place.

The emotional risks were great and the consequences immeasurable. But when I opened that suitcase, I made the decision that I was going to look carefully at my past without flinching, all in an effort to close the wounds that I thought would never heal.

Yes, I was curious to go back and reread the letters so I could mine them for details. But I was most eager to finally deal with the truth of my early life and how it affected the people I loved most. I owed it to my family to find out what really happened, to ask for the answers that my father could have provided but chose not to. How could I ignore the emotional freedom those answers would provide?

There's an old Yiddish proverb that says, "Man plans and God laughs." I fully understood the wisdom of that as I contemplated contacting my mother. I could see that despite my most careful planning, the road of life was totally unpredictable. I always thought *I* was doing the driving, with my destination strategies all planned out. But my settled life had been upended. Fate had provided unanticipated good fortune, even a heart-to-heart connection that had come out of the blue. That's what I had hoped for.

There I was, on the brink of initiating a message to my mother, a message whose outcome I could not control. But I had to go for it. If I didn't, I'd live with regret for the rest of my life.

———————

IT TOOK SEVERAL WEEKS to work up the courage, but I finally wrote my mother a letter, which I've excerpted below.

January 24, 1997

Dear Mrs. Hoffman,

This will obviously come as a shock to you but I believe I am your son, Ed, born . . . in Los Angeles, California. For all these years, I believed that you had passed away in childbirth sometime in 1939 as my father had told me. His was not a simple life and when he died in 1971, he left a suitcase which I did not fully go through until late last year. There was enough information there to indicate that you did not die and could be living given your age when I was born. I subsequently hired a search agency and gave them the shreds of evidence that I had which included a letter from you to Dad. . . To their and my surprise, they were able to locate you in a matter of weeks.

This is not a simple situation, but if you are willing I would like to visit you in the very near future. Since so many years have passed you may decide this is something you may not want to reopen. If this is the case, I will understand and respect your decision. On the other hand, if you would welcome a visit, I suggest that if it is convenient for you, my wife, Barbara, and I will come to St. Louis on February 2. You should know that on this side of the family, you have three grandchildren and two great-grandchildren!!

Looking forward to speaking with you,

Ed

I also gave her my phone number and invited her to call me, but only if she felt ready. I set a time and date—6:00 p.m. on a specified night. Either she would or wouldn't call.

On the night I suggested, I waited for my mother's call like an anxious boy, but the phone never rang. I was crestfallen.

Sensing my deep disappointment, Barbara sent me out to pick up dinner for the family as if it were just another night at home. While I was gone, that's when the phone rang! Lo and behold, there was my mother. She and Barbara talked and instantly connected. It was as if they had known each other all their lives.

When I got home, Barbara was all excited, sharing the news that my mother had called and that they had had a very warm conversation. Honestly, for a brief moment, I felt weak in the knees. I was overcome with a flood of emotion that I hadn't ever felt before and haven't felt since. It was a combination of incredible excitement and relief blended with fear. What would it be like to talk to my actual mother? It was an encounter that would answer so many questions, scary as it might be to confront the events of the past.

It took a few minutes for me to collect myself and call her back. As she picked up the phone and said hello, it was strange yet lovely to hear her voice. She openly told me that she'd gotten remarried and had another son, Phil, a physician practicing in Lexington, Kentucky, who was the father of three sons of his own.

On the call, my mother was very calm and matter-of-fact, friendly but not very emotional. Neither was I. In fact, I had set a minimal goal, which was simply to talk to her and eventually meet but not necessarily become totally involved in her life. As I look back on it now, I can see that this was a defense mechanism.

Yet there was so much to discuss and learn about each other. That was the exciting part. And still, I knew in my heart that neither one of us was looking to rekindle the mother-son relationship. Frankly, I didn't want it. That would have been too much pressure at that early stage, though our relationship ultimately did become much closer. In my initial thinking, there was too much distance between us in terms of time and expectations to recreate a family bond. Bottom line: I didn't want to disrupt my life.

Besides, Barbara's mother, Mae, had treated me like a son from the day Barbara and I married. Mae had been the only true mother figure I'd ever known. We were similar in temperament in so many ways and had become very close. In fact, over the years I felt as if she adopted me every bit as much as I adopted her. I didn't want to shake the foundation of that relationship or upset the familial peace we generally enjoyed.

But if Sophie were willing to share her memories with me, I was open to taking the relationship a step further. Before hanging up, I asked her if she'd like to meet face-to-face, and she was totally receptive to it. So I arranged a trip to St. Louis!

ON THE DAY I WAS TO MEET MY MOTHER IN PERSON, coincidentally, there was a headline on the front page of the *St. Louis*

Post-Dispatch that read ***Girl Finds Mother After 27 Years!*** I had to smile because I intended to keep the miracle of my own reunion with my mother quiet—not like the public spectacle in the newspaper. Yes, the St. Louis girl had waited twenty-seven years for a reunion, but I had waited *fifty-seven*—a full thirty years longer. It was still a shock to my system, so I didn't want anyone besides Barbara to know why I was in St. Louis. Understandably, I was still uncomfortable, quite nervous, and apprehensive about the whole scenario. I stood outside my mother's apartment door for a good minute or two before finally ringing the bell. I was oddly fearful that once that door opened, I'd be taking on an obligation I didn't need or wouldn't be able to get out of. What if I decided it wasn't for me?

"I still have time to walk away," I told myself. But then I raised my forefinger and pressed the button. My heart was racing with anticipation.

When my mother answered and I was a foot away from her, it was overwhelming.

"It's your son, fifty-seven years late!" I quipped.

Though I hadn't seen her for all those decades, I instantly felt a sense of recognition. It was like an out-of-body experience, totally surreal, especially because there was a physical likeness between the two of us that caught me off guard.

We didn't hug initially. After all, we were total strangers. There was no weeping or wailing; no drama at all. She just invited me in, and I stepped into her small two-bedroom apartment.

Throughout my entire life, I had imagined my mother to be a dark-haired beauty, like the glamorous ladies I saw on the movie screen, with perfectly set hair, a great figure, and impeccable taste in clothes. But as it turned out, my mother was an ordinary woman—like any other mom. She was rather short, like me. I had to press a reset button in my mind and discard my childhood fantasies. This was real life.

My mother spoke articulately, as if she was well educated, and she talked very quickly, which shocked me because I recognized that trait in myself. Suddenly, I wasn't just all my father.

To make the afternoon even more sociable, my mother invited her son, Phil, whom she had had with Mr. Hoffman, and one of Phil's sons, Mark. She also invited two of her nieces, Lois and Judy (who were three and four years older than I was, respectively), to join our reunion. During our time together in St. Louis, they were the ones who looked after me. That afternoon, they were all eager to gather at Sophie's and greet me. As my mother spoke openly about her parents and siblings, she described the family relationship as quite dysfunctional, just as I described it earlier. She didn't even know the whereabouts of two of her five siblings, having lost touch with them at a very young age.

We sat in the living room and talked for hours. My mother showed me pictures of me as a baby with her nieces when they were six and seven years old. And there they were in the room with me, two ladies in their sixties. It turned out to be quite an afternoon!

I had brought along a video of my twenty-fifth wedding anniversary celebration so I could give Sophie a glimpse into my own family life. As we eased into a slightly more comfortable rapport, I showed her the video, then began asking her more about my father, their relationship, and what happened between them. This was key to me.

From Sophie's point of view, not surprisingly, her relationship with my father was quite toxic. He was difficult, demanding, and had trouble holding a job. He had a violent temper and treated her as a servant rather than his wife. He was old school in that he wanted my mother to cook, clean, and take care of him and me. Most detrimentally, he wanted to control her—what she did, how she dressed, and what she ate. All in all, she felt threatened by him, especially on the day he kidnapped me. He told her that he was going to keep me, that she would never get me back, and that she shouldn't even bother looking for us. As she spoke, I got a sense that he made it very clear he would somehow hurt her if she came after me. She was frightened of him and didn't believe that calling the police and asking them to help find me would do any good.

At that point in her life, Sophie had no financial resources to resist my father or hire a lawyer to track him down, even though she had full

Brad and Marthe's New Year's Eve wedding, Denver, CO (2005)

Brad with Sophie and Ruth at his wedding (2005)

Boat trip to the Grenadines (2005)

My seventieth birthday party at the Big Easy in Montana with Phil and Nancy (2006)

At dedication of the Hajim School of Engineering (2009)

At dedication ceremony with President Joel Seligman and family (2009)

Hawaii (2010)

Queenwood Golf Club with Ocean Reef friends (2010)
Photo credit: Cary Hazelgrove

My seventy-fifth birthday (2011)
Photo credit: Cary Hazelgrove

Nantucket with five of our eight grandchildren (2011)
Photo credit: Cary Hazelgrove

With my golf partner Lynn Rotando at Card
Sound Club in Ocean Reef (2012)

Ra'am's college graduation from UC, Santa Barbara (2015)

Our fiftieth wedding anniversary at The Point, Saranac Lake, New York (2015)

With president Joel Seligman and provost Rob Clark
at University of Rochester graduation (May 2014)

My family celebrating at the Horatio Alger award ceremony (2015)

*With family at the University of Rochester dedication of
the statue of me in the Engineering Quadrangle (2016)*

*With my scholarship student, Sarah
Walters, at her PhD ceremony (May 2019)*

legal custody of me. In some way, she implied that she didn't have the resources to care for me and thought that perhaps my father did.

Back in 1939, remember, there she was, a twenty-four-year-old single mom. Her parents weren't interested in supporting her or me. They rejected us, leaving my mother to fend for herself. At that point, she had no possible way of standing up to my father. She went about her life as if nothing happened—just as my father and I went on with ours.

My mother told me on our first weekend together (and many times thereafter) that she wasn't actually angry about my father taking me because in her heart, she felt I was probably better off with him. This astonished me. What mother would willingly comply with being separated from a three-year-old child?

But in her mind, she wouldn't have been able to give me all the advantages he could, so it turned out for the best. Perhaps this rationale was a defense against the immense sadness she felt. She also told me she thought I did better in my life because of it, and if I had stayed with her I would not have been able to accomplish all the things I did. While my father's decision to take me was made out of pure emotion—driven by possessiveness and revenge—perhaps my mother's decision was made out of pure reason. One parent was feeling and not thinking, and the other was thinking and not feeling—or at least not allowing herself to feel. Both of them had acted strangely.

My mother's admission was certainly stunning.

———

THAT VISIT WAS THE BEGINNING of a warm and satisfying twelve-year relationship. I called her every Sunday, visited her regularly, and had her come to our house in Greenwich many times. She went on family vacations with us and spent almost every holiday with us. In short, we really loved her and drew her into our family in a way that I might not have initially expected. She was so warm and undemanding, opening her heart to a brand-new family.

Still, she frequently said she understood that she was really *not* my mother because she didn't spend time raising me. She didn't remember basic things about me as an infant and toddler—including, for example, whether she breastfed me. Even so, if I missed a Sunday call, she would joke the next Sunday, "Long time between drinks of water!" Jewish guilt—she had it down like a mother!

She also confided that before I contacted her, she was ready to leave this world. But once I came along, it gave her a reason to hang around. Yes, she already had a son and three grandchildren, but I think our reunion ignited a new spark in her. At last, she met the child she had lost, and she became part of our future. It was really kind of amazing.

By the way, she had told my half brother, Phil, about her first marriage but not about my existence until I reached out to her. But when she finally did, she said, "Remember that brother you always wanted to have? Well, I have one for you now!"

Sophie had a wonderful sense of humor and, like me, was always ready to tell a good joke, sometimes a little off-color. She got along extremely well with Barbara's mother and aunt, Ruth, and the three women became very good friends. In St. Louis, we threw an eighty-fifth birthday party for her, followed five years later by a ninetieth. I wasn't surprised when she put on high heels and drank martinis for the occasion. She loved attention—she was president of Hadassah, active in her synagogue, and active in the Jewish community.

Shortly after the party for her ninetieth birthday, Sophie began to decline, so Phil moved her into an assisted living facility. She died peacefully in 2008, at the age of ninety-three. I have the gift of having known her in her final years, which means the world to me and Barbara. I guess I never felt what I would call love for my *mother*. From my earliest years, I'd always been highly protective of myself, guarded about my emotions, with a shield firmly in place. Maybe I take after my mother in that way: she was a very practical, unsentimental person. She had no use for drama. True, there were a couple of times when our eyes welled up if we were talking about old times, but we never shed any significant tears. Besides, I really didn't know how to handle motherly love. I felt awkward when Mae or Sophie attempted to show me such love. In some unconscious way, I guess I thought it was either not real or might be taken away. I didn't want to get attached or involved. And I never wanted help accepting motherly love. To this day, I have trouble asking for help, which in many ways is a significant weakness. But in the end, I knew that both Sophie and Mae loved me, and it was their affection that helped me heal and put the past behind me.

My half brother, Phil, is a warm and wonderful person, and we have become close as brothers, talking regularly and seeing each other a few times a year. His wife, Nancy, and Barbara have become good friends, too. His children—Ben, Scott, and Mark—and mine have also gotten to know one another, and one of them is quite close to Corey. Phil will not let more than two weeks go by without calling, but we do live different lives in different places. Even the closest of siblings who grew up together could say that.

As I look back on the entire chapter of our lives with Sophie, I believe that our efforts to integrate her into our family slowly and carefully were successful. One sad note: six months after we introduced Sophie to Mae, Mae suffered a bad fall and never really recovered from it. Her health declined slowly until she died at the age of ninety-eight, in 2005. For all intents and purposes, Mae had been my mother since the day I married Barbara. She was a source of total support and love. You could tell her anything. Sometimes I wonder if Sophie's arrival might have had a negative effect on her, though they liked each other and got along. In any case, I had at that point lost two mothers, but I would always be grateful for what both of them gave me.

At the Nantucket Golf Club Groundbreaking (1994)

CHAPTER EIGHTEEN

Red Letter Day:
August 27, 1997

c: 1997–1999

W HILE I WAS ADJUSTING to a new relationship with my mother, I was also quite consumed at work, with buying back Furman Selz from Xerox, and continued to get involved in a number of charitable activities.

Most significant, I became a trustee of Greenwich Hospital and ran its endowment. In addition, John Hill Wilson and I cochaired the major gift committee for a capital campaign to essentially rebuild the hospital so it could retain its accreditation. With the help of the entire community and a dedicated board, we raised the first $50 million. We were succeeded by the superbly capable Nancy Lynch, who led the second, even bigger campaign. The $150 million renovation turned the hospital into a real community asset. I ran the endowment for twelve years, after which I passed the baton to Alan Breed, a well-known money manager.

At around the same time, I was elected to the board of the Harvard Business School Alumni Association. Then, after serving six years, I was voted in as president. During my term, we put a major emphasis on lifelong learning—the creation of a number of courses for alumni. The one I am most proud of is The Entrepreneur's Tool Kit, which Myra

Hart, with a little help from me, made into a very successful course. After Professor Lynda Applegate took it over, it became one of the most successful executive education programs in the curriculum.

I'm also proud to say that when my term was up I was instrumental in backing the candidacy of Susan Good (MBA '71) as the association's next president—the first female president in the organization's history. She is very special and was by far the most qualified person for the position. After finishing my term on the alumni board, I was elected to the Dean Advisory Council, which is the body that functions like the board for the Harvard Business School. I stepped down from the DAC in 2008 when I assumed the chairmanship of the board of trustees at the University of Rochester, since their meetings were held on the exact same dates. Former dean of HBS, Kim Clark, agreed that I should take the position at Rochester because I could probably make a greater difference there. I nonetheless remained active at HBS, chairing my forty-fifth, fiftieth, and fifty-fifth reunions and in each case raising a record amount of money, with the fiftieth's $37 million record yet to be surpassed. I must give credit to David Wolff and Tim Day, my chairs of major gifts, and to classmates like Ron Agel (who took us over the top in both the fiftieth and the fifty-fifth), Sammy Lee, Rahul Bajaj, and Dick Corbett, who made major commitments. We achieved these records after losing three of our most generous classmates, George Baker, Ed Linde, and Peter Sacerdote. Peter had also cochaired a number of reunions with me, and his wife, Bonnie, has continued to make generous donations in his memory. None of this could have been accomplished without our reunion team: Dorsey Dunn, Stenner Sweeney, Leo Swergold, John Humphrey, Tim Litle, Joan Griewank Colligan, Gracie Fritzinger, Mal Salter, and many others.

AFTER THE NEWLY INDEPENDENT FURMAN SELZ had paid off a large part of its debt, completing its "slimming down" phase, we were set to go into 1997 leaner, meaner, and in very good financial shape.

We were even planning to move our offices, leasing four floors at 280 Park Avenue, a more prestigious building only a few blocks from our existing office.

Although I was rather bullish at the start of 1997, by the middle of the year, I began to get that old familiar feeling that things in the market were going to get a little uncomfortable. Call it instinct, intuition, or raw gut feeling. It's an inner voice that I never doubt—whether it's telling me something good or bad. It comes from the accumulation of experience and the ability to recognize when a pattern is beginning to form.

For example, I collect what I call anecdotal evidence. Let's say people are buying big, expensive apartments and works of art and seemingly overpaying for them. That happens at the top of the market, not at the bottom. Paintings sell for many times what they sold for a few years earlier. Companies are being bought for ridiculous prices. People are generally overspending. All these things indicate that there may be trouble just ahead.

In 1997, all of Furman Selz's competitors were being taken over, mainly by overseas financial institutions. I watched as Montgomery Securities, Robertson Stephens, Alex. Brown & Sons, and Oppenheimer all got swallowed up in a relatively short period of time.

Were we next?

In the past, I might have said no. But in 1997, in that uncertain market, I wasn't so sure.

Furman Selz's equity capital was then around $100 million, up from $26 million when we bought the firm back in '92. Even so, we were by no means considered competitive anymore, because our rivals all had big backers and could do things we could not do.

Once again, the call came from my Furman Selz bankers that we had better sell out. But I had that instinctive gut feeling to wait, just as we did before. I thought our patience would pay off.

How?

I had already secretly fielded one bid to buy the company for $400 million, which did not feel like a good fit, so I kept it hidden from everyone except Steve. In order for us to sell again, the deal had to be right.

There were two things I insisted on. First, I did not want to work for anyone else or, at the very least, I wanted to be sure we would be as independent as possible. Second, if we were going to seriously entertain an offer, there had to be more to it than big money to get my attention. For one thing, it had to be a good strategic fit. The acquiring company had to have what we needed to be competitive and take us to the next level—in other words, capital and an international presence. In addition, the company had to give us a high degree of autonomy so we could carry out our plans.

IN SEPTEMBER OF 1997, ING (Internationale Nederlanden Groep), a large Dutch financial institution that was founded in 1991, lost out in its quest for Montgomery Securities. It subsequently hired an investment bank to find another strong US partner to acquire.

It turned out we were on its bankers' short list.

When they did their due diligence, they discovered we were almost as large as Montgomery. Much to their surprise, our product line was actually more diverse and thus more of a fit. Although Montgomery was a very strong firm, it was almost totally focused on tech clients. We had positions in five or six major industries and had a $12 billion money-management business. As they began peeling away the layers of our company, it suddenly became very attractive to them.

Things were moving fast, so I hired an investment banker, and in less than thirty days we had a deal in final negotiation. By any standard, this was considered very fast. Although I asked for $600 million, ING offered $500 million. I knew they wanted the company, and they finally acquiesced during an intense back-and-forth, face-to-face negotiation.

The price was actually $725 million, because we had $125 million in debt on our balance sheet at the time. ING was paying nearly seven times book value, at or near a record price paid for an investment bank.

Like the Xerox deal, the transaction was structured in all cash, my preferred method of payment. I allocated $500 million of it for present shareholders and $100 million of it for non-shareholders or small shareholders as retention contracts. I also structured the deal so that payout of the purchase price would be staggered over a period of three years, the same way I did with the Xerox deal. The extended payout period was not only fair to ING but also gave our management a chance to adjust to being part of a large organization.

ING paid two-thirds up-front and the final third at the end of the third year. By having ING hold back the final third of the payment, I ensured that most people would stay with the firm long enough to get their share of the payment, which was sizable. Over this period, we could grow the firm, so that if some people left there would be new people to take their places.

Throughout our negotiations, ING's overriding message was *local presence, global reach.*

It sure sounded good, and it had me hooked, because it solved the two major problems I foresaw for Furman Selz: our need for capital and growing need for international capabilities. Both were necessary next steps. ING executives told me that Furman Selz would remain independent, and I took them at their word—unfortunately.

ING occupied sixteen floors at 55 East 52nd Street, right down the block from where we were already located, so our new lease (the one at 280 Park Avenue) became a nice asset, which they eventually sold at what I believe was a profit.

We closed the deal in less than sixty days, on August 27, 1997.[6] The selling of the firm, you could say, brought closure to my business life. We started with seventy people in 1983 and created a company of eight hundred employees in fourteen years. We went from $20 million in revenue to nearly $500 million, and we sold the firm for a very favorable price, rewarding more than two hundred people for their efforts. I did what I hoped I might do, and it came out better than I could have ever expected.

---

[6] For further details, see the aforementioned Harvard Business School case study, "A Tale of Two Acquisitions."

UNFORTUNATELY, in a very short amount of time, 45 days, ING changed the management that oversaw our division. Like a dentist who looks in a new patient's mouth and asks, "Who did *this* work?," the new manager reported that ING had decided to integrate its US operations with the operations of its subsidiary ING Barings, based in New York. And I was to become the cochairman of the fused three-part organization.

I vehemently objected. "This setup will never work," I said.

I wrote a long memorandum trying to convince ING that it was making a mistake. Next, I went to Amsterdam to plead my case. ING resisted and said it still wanted me to merge our group. But I reiterated that it would be extremely difficult and deleterious to us, and even more so for ING. Trying to put three different cultures together was impossible.

My pleas fell on deaf ears. ING owned us, and because I was a good soldier, all I could do was try to do what it directed me to do. I got busy putting together an integration committee while working with a consultant to make the transition as smooth as possible.

In just a few months, my suspicions were more than confirmed. I told ING that I would help but I could not manage the ING Barings–Furman Selz group. Why? Because ING's operation in New York already had two different cultures, and it was almost impossible to blend in a third culture, especially because the ING and Barings cultures had not yet meshed.

I negotiated a deal whereby I would manage the new money-management division, called ING Furman Selz Asset Management, and temporarily act as a figurehead for the entire operation while still holding some responsibility for the rest of Furman Selz.

Voilà! Problem solved for me, but not for my team. I was unhappy with the decision, but there was little I could do.

My first big brouhaha with the executives at the home office in Amsterdam came at bonus time in 1998, when the ING Barings group lost $1 billion or so trading emerging-market debt. That group's performance had nothing to do with our division, but because Amsterdam viewed us as part of ING Barings, it meant no or very little bonus money.

Obviously, that decision didn't go over very well. I had to go to war to get at least something for our people. Management eventually compromised, but their reluctance started our relationship off on the worst possible footing.

Yes, it was the right time to sell Furman Selz to ING. But as in any such transaction, once you sell, you give up control, even if you think you know how things *will* be managed. Foreign companies especially have trouble understanding US companies and the way we do business—and vice versa. I always made it a priority to look closely at the *culture* of a potential new partner. Does it fit? Does it meld? Considerations about compensation and lifestyle expectations vary tremendously, so I always vetted those in advance of accepting any offer. Language can often be a barrier. In fact, even when you speak the same language, meaning and interpretation are quite subjective. I must admit I misjudged the culture of ING and what might happen if its management were to change, which it did.

Perhaps my biggest revelation after the sale was the difference in our people's dedication and performance when we were independent versus owned by someone else. This should not have surprised me, but I was taken aback by the speed of the change.

ON THE HOME FRONT, in 1990, after Barbara and I bought our lot in Nantucket, a friend of ours there encouraged us to apply to the Nantucket Yacht Club and the Sankaty Head Golf Club. We thought we would enjoy both, so we applied while our new house was being built. I thought getting into the clubs would be easy. After all, I sat next to the commodore of the yacht club on the University of Rochester board of trustees—a position to which I had been elected two years earlier, in

1988—and the person who sponsored us for the golf club was loved by everyone in the community.

But after *four years* on the waiting list, we were rejected by both clubs! The letter I received from the yacht club went a step further and asked us not to reapply. I was astounded. During those years, Barbara was on the board of the Nantucket Historical Association, and I was on the board of the Nantucket Conservation Foundation, two of the most important organizations on the island.

What could possibly have been the reason? I couldn't imagine. The person who sponsored us for membership in the golf club was very upset. The moment I got the rejection letter from the golf club, I said to Barbara, "We're not going to get into any clubs, so let's sell the house and leave the island. If I can't play golf, I don't want to be here. Let's just forget about Nantucket." A knee-jerk reaction, I admit.

Barbara loved Nantucket and did not want to leave. She reminded me that when we bought our property in Vail, around 1988, I had been one of the twenty founders of a beautiful golf club there, Eagle Springs, which was a big success. I was also involved in the founding of the Game Creek Club in Vail, up on a mountain. "If you did that, why can't you build a golf course on Nantucket?" she asked.

"Because there's no available land here," I replied. "It's a very different story in Vail."

The more we talked about it, though, the more appealing the idea seemed. It was a little crazy, and wildly ambitious, but if I could find the right parcel of land on Nantucket, why not? I confess that there was also a little voice in the back of my mind, the revenge factor, saying, "That'll show 'em."

In early 1994, we called our real estate agent, Mimi Merton, and as luck would have it, two parcels of land, around three hundred acres each, were for sale. I couldn't believe there was that much available land on the island. Our real estate agent did some research, however, and it looked like only one of those lots was truly on the market.

The owners of that land were members of the famous Coffin family, a group of whalers operating out of Nantucket from the seventeenth to the nineteenth centuries, when that industry dominated the island. The Coffins owned a huge swath of land on Nantucket and had been selling some of it off from the time the patriarch of the family died in 1994, because the real estate and inheritance taxes were so high.

I called Fred Green, who had put together everything we needed to build our course in Vail, and asked him to look at the property. He came to Nantucket, and we drove my Jeep along the dirt paths that cut through the land. The scrub oak was as tall as the car. I had to stand on the roof to look around, but we both could see the course in our minds.

"What do you think?" I asked. Fred was all in.

Walter Forbes joined us, and a short time later we added three more board members: Howard Clark, Joe Welch, and Bob Greenhill.

We then needed to raise money. A mere three weeks later, we had rounded up fifty people who put in $200,000 each to become founders. (I can't resist mentioning the story of one prospect who, when I called, told me he was interested but asked if he could discuss it with his wife first. I said no—and he said, "Okay, count me in!" We laugh about it to this day.)

That meant we had $10 million—$2 million more than we needed to buy the land. After some tense negotiation, we closed the sale. At the time, it was the largest amount ever paid per inland acre for land on Nantucket. Many thought that we were crazy and the project would fail. Over the course of the following six months, we sold 250 more memberships, raising $45 million before we moved a single shovel of dirt! Obviously, there was large latent demand for a golf course on the island. When the course and club opened on August 27, 1997—coincidentally, the exact same day we announced the sale of Furman Selz to ING—the original founders got most of their money back. This was the deal, since they took the risk that we may not have gotten the permitting required and would not have been able to build the course. We said, "If it gets built, and there is money left over, it will be split among the founders."

The Nantucket Golf Club, as we named it, was brilliantly designed by Rees Jones and voted the country's best new private golf course of

1998 according to *Golf Digest* magazine. That year, the clubhouse was also rated the best new clubhouse by Crittenden Golf, Inc. In *Golf* magazine's 2000–2001 list of the top 100 modern courses in America, the Nantucket Golf Club ranked number 50; in its list of the top 100 courses in the world that same year, we ranked number 98. (Barbara had certainly been right in encouraging me to do this!)

There are club members from all over the country who still thank me for building the club because they wouldn't have stayed on Nantucket otherwise. Some of their spouses are especially grateful. In a sense, we changed the image of the island for those people, probably even helping to increase the value of Nantucket real estate overall.

Beyond the recognition, the experience of building a golf course, watching it come to life from the ground up, was immensely gratifying. It was amazing how a bunch of bulldozers digging into the earth could ultimately create such a magical place where great things could happen—truly art created by bulldozers. On the list of my proudest accomplishments, the golf club certainly ranks way up there—although the actual building and the success of its management must be credited almost solely to the genius and hard work of our partner, Fred Green. A few years later, I was also one of the founders of a magnificent new course that he built outside of London, called Queenwood.

I won't deny that I enjoy being member number one, especially when I'm asked for my membership number at the snack bar. I often think that if the other club hadn't rejected me, we would have never built our own and would have missed out on this rare opportunity. As I've learned, when someone rejects you, it may be a blessing in disguise. Sometimes things have a *reason* for happening, one that can't precisely be determined. I was lucky to be rejected—how does that sound?

In 2002, we established the Children's Charity Classic at the Nantucket Golf Club, an annual golf tournament and auction that benefit children on the island. The Nantucket Golf Club Foundation may now be the largest charitable institution on the island, possibly the largest in the island's history. We field more than fifty grant applications annually and contribute to almost every charity on

Nantucket. We also have put more than twenty Nantucket High School graduates through college and recently have established a vocational school scholarship program. As if our real estate adventures on Nantucket weren't enough, it was around this time that Barbara and I decided to build a house on that beautiful piece of waterfront property in Key Largo, Florida, that we had bought back in 1988. That house, on Snapper Point Drive, became our primary family home and remains so to this day. It has everything we could want—room for the family, water views, and nearly perfect weather in the winter months.

———————————

AS I SETTLED INTO MY NEW ROLE as CEO of ING Furman Selz Asset Management, my mandate was to integrate the ING and Furman Selz money-management operations. I still had some responsibility for the rest of ING's New York operation, too, especially in compensation and strategic matters.

In 1999, ING Furman Selz Asset Management had one of the best years ever, earning around $200 million in our little division. This essentially paid ING back for any overpayment it thought it may have made in acquiring our firm. We earned so much money that year that some of my bonus pool had to be deferred so that it would not embarrass my new boss.

ING continued with its US acquisition binge, buying ReliaStar Life Insurance and Aetna Financial Services. Every time ING bought a company, we got the investment management part of the business. For example, ReliaStar added around $10 billion in assets; Aetna added another $20 billion. We made some acquisitions of our own, too, and by 2001 we had $60 billion under management. The assets came in so fast that it was hard to manage the growth. I went from having a couple of reporting entities to having twelve.

When the market did very poorly in late 2000 and 2001, our profitability, like everyone else's, went down. Amsterdam's solution was to send in a fourth manager, and it put in a new chairman for the parent company, the third since the Furman Selz acquisition.

In 2002, I was sixty-six years old, which was four years past ING's standard retirement age. After some discussion, my new boss and I decided it was probably time for me to leave. I wanted to buy back part of Furman Selz, but we were too far apart on price and process. ING thought I was gaming it, but I wasn't. The parts I wanted to buy all eventually left the company, and ING received little to nothing for them. Just before I left the group, ING's combined banking operations, including that of Furman Selz, started to lose a substantial amount of money. ING sold the division to ABN AMRO, a large Dutch banking institution, for a bargain price. This relationship lasted just a year. ABN eventually closed it down, a sad ending to a lot of hard work.

Meanwhile, my separation from ING was pretty amicable, with a fairly generous severance package and only a one-year noncompete clause. I could not work with anyone who had more than $500 million under management. It wasn't a big request, and it wasn't a problem for me to honor it.

Father and daughter team (2012)

CHAPTER NINETEEN

Marketus: An Ornery Bear

c. 2002–2016

F OR ME, BEING IDLE IS UNACCEPTABLE. It's both boring and unproductive. And I've always thought that one has to remain productive and engaged in *something*. Golf isn't enough.

After I left ING, I asked myself that same old question: "What's next?" I knew I wasn't ready to hang up my gloves just yet. Against my better judgment, I decided to start a hedge fund, and thus my new venture, MLH Capital, was born (more on the derivation of the name in a moment).

By this time, Barbara and I had been living in Greenwich for thirty-three years. Our kids were all adults and living on their own. Barbara decided it was finally time to sell our house and move to New York City, where my commute to the office would be much easier.

This was just after 9/11, and a lot of people were moving *out* of the city. But Barbara, with foresight, said this was the time to move in. I protested, "That's crazy—all my smart friends expect another terrorist incident, and my golf course is here in Greenwich."

But as usual, Barbara prevailed, and she found a beautiful apartment in the River House, a historic 1931 art deco building facing the East River at 52nd Street, with eleven-foot ceilings and sweeping views. Pete Peterson, in fact, once owned an apartment there, and its most famous occupant is Henry Kissinger.

Our duplex apartment, on the sixteenth and seventeenth floors, was perfect, with three bedrooms and almost four thousand square feet of terrace space—almost as large as the interior. It was as close to being like our home in Greenwich as possible, with the same sense of warmth, spacious rooms, and impressive vistas.

The apartment had a mahogany-paneled library; a huge dining room to its west, perfect for family entertaining; and three very large bedrooms on the upper level, each with its own bath. The views were spectacular, and there was more than enough room for our children and their growing families to visit. Real estate prices had come down in the city quite a bit after 9/11, and after we sold our house in Greenwich, what little we had left over went into redecorating.

WHEN I FORMED MLH CAPITAL, I chose as my partners Jon Wimbish, a thirty-five-year-old analyst who worked for me at ING, and Adam Johnson, a trader at ING whom I had known forever. I also hooked up again with Steve Blecher, who agreed to handle my back-office work. Steve had recently joined a group of ex–Furman Selz employees to establish a financial services firm. Heading it up was Fred Joseph, the former CEO of Drexel Burnham Lambert, and John Morgan, the former head of corporate finance at ING Barings, who together formed Morgan Lewins, later changing the name to Morgan Joseph & Company, Inc. (no relation to Morgan Stanley). The MLH in MLH Capital, thus, stands for "Morgan Lewins Hajim." I took the twenty-fifth floor at 600 Fifth Avenue, the same building they were in, overlooking the skating rink at Rockefeller Center.

In no time and much to Barbara's chagrin, I was off and running on this new entrepreneurial venture, violating all the rules I had long ago established, including "Never start anything from scratch." As I had done at Greenwich Management, I started a business without a platform—without minimum critical mass. I knew better. But I told myself that things would be different this time. After all, running this hedge fund would be just like managing my own money, which I had always done.

I started two funds: the Marketus Growth Fund and the Marketus Income Fund. (Marketus was my nom de plume during the many years I wrote strategy pieces for Furman Selz.) I was the only one who knew that the Marketus funds bore a strong resemblance to Greenwich Management's old Growth Fund of America and Income Fund of America.

I started the fund with some of my own money and some from accounts that I managed for family and friends. But much to my surprise, some of my closest friends declined to invest with me, which did not make me happy. Ultimately, I started with between $50 and $60 million. I figured I would just have a good time investing—I wasn't interested in making any effort to build up the fund. And I let everyone know this in advance.

We did quite well the first year. When the market was down, we were up. Our numbers were looking very good the second year, too. The market was up, and we were up with it.

Money starting flowing in, and soon the fund was up over $100 million. Still, I refused to market it. Nevertheless, because some of the young people in the office wanted more growth, I hired a junior marketing person and allowed one of our analysts to work with him on marketing the fund. Their efforts failed and the analyst subsequently left the firm.

I had made a big mistake: it's my belief that when an analyst gets involved in marketing, it hurts his ability to totally focus on his work as an analyst. After all, if you're a brain surgeon, you shouldn't operate on hearts. In retrospect, I should have hired a professional marketing person or a top-notch marketing firm if I wanted to market the fund.

My partner Jon and I labored on through '04, '05, and '06. We were doing a little better than the market, and then I started to get bearish. The old feeling came up again. Maybe I was getting tired or, as Barbara says, maybe I just didn't want to worry about other people's money. Perhaps I wanted to do something simpler with my life after all.

———————

IT WAS AROUND THIS TIME when the University of Rochester, my alma mater, came to me and asked me to assist it with a presidential search. I participated in that effort, and in 2005 we hired Joel Seligman, who had been the dean of the Washington University School of Law.

In 2007, Joel called and asked to take me to dinner. I thought he wanted to thank me for my years of service on the board of trustees. Instead, much to my shock, he asked me to become the board's chairman. That stopped me in my tracks. I had given generously to the university over the years and had been involved with it in several ways (see chapter 18). But becoming the chair of the board was a whole new level of commitment.

On the one hand, I thought Joel's request might be divine intervention. There I was, growing somewhat weary of the hedge fund, even though it was doing well. It would be a good time to leave the business.

On the other hand, when I told Jon that I was considering taking the job and that if I did, he would have to step up and take charge, he told me it was the last thing he wanted to do. I was flabbergasted: I thought he was fully qualified and had the experience and demeanor necessary to succeed.

Jon explained that he liked working for me, coming in every day and doing research, but he didn't want to take the reins. I had mistakenly projected something on him, something that was not in his heart. In fact, the idea of leading the company terrified him so much that a few months later he left to become the CFO of a small oil company, leaving money management altogether, which came as another surprise. He was a great partner and I was sorry to see him leave. With his leaving and my considering the job as chair, it was obviously time for a change.

———————

BEING BEARISH IN 2007—which, in retrospect, was remarkably clairvoyant—but being underinvested resulted in the fund's being flat for the year, thus underperforming the market.

This resulted in some redemptions, which disappointed me. After all, we had done so well over the previous five-year period. But this turn of events made me decide to close the funds.

My small team pleaded with me to at least keep one fund open and give them responsibility to manage a portion of it. I thought long and hard about what I wanted to do. Ultimately, I decided to close the income fund—and then I made a decision that was foolish, as I look back on it: I gave 40 percent of the growth fund to the two young guys who were with me. I told them that if they were down even 5 percent I would immediately close the fund.

As luck would have it, they started really well in early 2008 and were up quite nicely by midyear. By this time, however, I was an ornery bear. Still, they would not listen to my warnings. They were still up in August, before the financial world started unraveling. They tried to salvage themselves, but it was too late. By September, everything came apart, and we were down about 15 percent.

I took over the fund and tried to liquidate it. I even tried to manage my way through it with the idea of getting back some of our losses—a big mistake. Never try to manage your way out of a bear market if you are trying to liquidate a fund.

That was the end of the road. I allowed everyone to look for jobs while I liquidated the portfolio. I was at my first board meeting in Rochester as chair and spent most of the weekend on the phone selling stocks. It wasn't exactly the jubilant way I wanted to go into my fiftieth reunion weekend or the frame of mind I had hoped to have in my new role.

When I finished selling, I gave all the money back to the investors and received few if any complaints. After all, over the course of six years, we had outperformed the market by more than 5 percent per year. In the end, we closed out the year down around 20 percent, which wasn't bad, considering that the market was down by 37 percent.

I was angry with myself for not shutting things down when I wanted to. Also, my decision to close the fund was not smart. I still had around $70 million and a lot of very loyal investors. This taught me something I repeat to young people all the time: never make impulsive decisions out of anger, and never get down on yourself. It only results in even bigger and costlier mistakes.

When the dust finally settled in early 2009, all I had left was my assistant, Lillian Nahas, who had been with me for sixteen years, and too much office space. I shared the space with Bernard Selz and made arrangements to rent part of it to a young private equity manager, Brett Keith, and to Bob Israel, a longtime friend who was starting up a private equity fund focused on the oil industry. Brett and I first met at an HBS conference in Pittsburgh in 1999, when he was newly graduated from HBS and starting his own private equity fund. He asked me to invest $50,000 and wanted to use my name. I politely declined, but he was persistent during the three-day conference. Finally, I relented and went along with his proposition. Eighteen months later, he called and told me I had just made eighteen times my money on my investment. We have been friends and partners ever since.

I still had all my own money from the funds, plus a number of small investors who refused to leave. I had a daily job to go to.

The market finally turned in March of 2009, and thankfully I turned with it. In fact, I had one of my best years ever, which was wonderful for me, yet painful, because I might have done just as well with the fund and thus for my clients.

—————

IT WAS AT THIS TIME that my career took yet another turn. Bends in the road are predictable life occurrences and can be pretty comfortable if you just ride along with the flow. So that's exactly what I did.

Through one of the investment groups I was involved with—the Concept Group, which I cofounded in 1966—I met a young man, Mark Diker, who worked with his father, Chuck. The Dikers, along with another young man, Ross Koller, ran a series of hedge funds. These funds had done very well from 2003 to 2007, rising to $500 million from nothing. But when the market took its hit in 2008, the funds declined by about 50 percent and were being redeemed aggressively. The Harvard MBA–trained Mark needed some help, and he asked if I would take a look at their group. He said he and his father would sell me part of the company, and I could become its president.

At the time, although I was being wooed by a couple of other firms, there was nothing on the radar that tickled my fancy. Yes, I like to fix things, but I wasn't sure what I would be getting into with Diker Management, especially because it was a father-son operation. For an outsider, those are often slippery slopes to navigate.

After careful consideration, though, I felt that I could solve their problems, especially because I had seen most of the issues they were dealing with many times before. Besides, my lease at 600 Fifth Avenue was coming up, and I was going to have to move anyway.

While contemplating my decision, I brought up the opportunity to my YPO forum group, a monthly meeting of like-minded professionals who gather to discuss all things business and personal. (The group has been meeting regularly since 1977. When members reach the age of fifty, they "graduate" into either the World Presidents' Organization or the Chief Executives Organization, but the forums continue.)

Immediately the group warned me about joining a father-son company. Still, always game for a new challenge, I thought I could handle the family dynamics, especially because Chuck and I liked each other right off the bat. In addition, the company had an established platform. In that sense, it fulfilled one of my major requirements for a new venture. Diker Management also had to move to a new space, and I could take both Bob Israel's and Brett Keith's start-ups with me.

My daughter, Corey, who by then had graduated from the University of Vermont and received her MBA from Harvard Business School (a chip off the old block!), was working with me at MLH Capital as an analyst and as the manager of the family office part of the business. Fortunately, the Dikers said she could come with me as well. This was ideal. Within a few months, she was quickly hired by our new partners. Although I tried to discourage her from working with me, she saw this as a unique opportunity to work *with* and not necessarily *for* her old man.

When I joined Diker Management, I set about trying to solve some of its most urgent problems—specifically, a little lack of organization and structure, and a lack of marketing. The first things I did were to make some changes in the investment process, institute a risk-management system, and hire a person to do our marketing.

Then I went about raising money to invest. As part of my strategy, in 2011 we acquired Unterberg Management. That acquisition instantly doubled the size of Diker, from $200 million to $400 million. In the next two years, we produced record results in terms of performance and profitability. But almost from the beginning, the head of that firm, Tom Unterberg, was not comfortable and really never part of Diker management. Although I tried to help, he decided to leave in 2014, taking his funds with him. Given the small size of Diker, there was really not enough for me to do, and by 2016, once again I was contemplating another career move.

FLASHBACK TO 1982, when I was at Lehman Brothers and running the Lemco division. At that time, Pete Peterson called me and asked if I would be interested in having a young professor from the Harvard Business School, André Perold, sit in my space and observe my operations so he could write a case study of my management and investment strategies. Pete recommended this professor highly, so I agreed.[7]

I enjoyed having André in my department, and he did write a case on the company's practices. I got a chance to see my case taught at HBS, with me as the protagonist. Well, we kept in touch for many years after

---

[7] André later used the case study he wrote, "Lehman Management Co., Inc." (September 1983; case number 284–027), in his Harvard Business School classes.

that. In 2004, when I was at MLH Capital, he cofounded an asset management firm in Boston, HighVista Strategies, and a few years later, he asked me to become a member of the advisory board. He said all that was required was a trip to Boston once a year to participate in the meetings, so I agreed.

In 2015, André asked me if I was interested in becoming the nonexecutive chairman of the firm. At the time, I was still chairman of the board of trustees at the University of Rochester, and it needed nearly my full attention. After all, the university is a $4 billion, thirty-thousand-person operation. I thanked him but declined.

Fast-forward to 2016, when my term at the University of Rochester ended. Predictably, André called once again and repeated his offer. Our conversation was very brief. I asked, "What does the chairman do?" He facetiously replied, "Nothing." I said, "I'll take the job!" It has been a good experience for me, and André's "nothing" turned out to be a bit of an understatement, as I suspected.

In the fall of 2014, with no reason to stay in New York full-time anymore, Barbara and I sold our apartment in River House and bought a very small apartment on the West Side, on Central Park West, around five blocks from Corey and her three boys. Now Grandma can visit anytime!

LIKE ALL PARENTS, Barbara and I hoped for the best for our children. We wanted them to be happy, to prosper, and to achieve all their personal and professional goals. Of course, we made some mistakes—all parents do. But today, we're incredibly proud of our three children and eight grandchildren (ranging in age from seven to twenty-seven). We didn't bring our children up to follow any particular religion or life philosophy, but we instilled in them the value of hard work and the importance of giving to others. The joy they have given us in return is beyond measure.

Our oldest, G. B., is a filmmaker, though he entered the University of California, San Diego, as a physics major. He was a strong math and science student, but he found his love in the arts and switched his major to fine arts. After graduation, he pursued his dreams by getting a master's degree in film production.

Like his parents, who love warm weather, G. B. has lived in Hilo, Hawaii, for the past twenty-five years. You might say his home is a combination movie production studio and tropical farm. Hawaii is also the ideal place for him to pursue his passion for scuba diving, which combines two of his other loves—underwater life and film.

He and his ex-wife, Karen Akiba, have three boys—Ra'am, Noam, and Luka. Ra'am, our eldest grandson, graduated from the University of California, Santa Barbara, and is presently working in San Francisco as an environmental consultant.

There is a saying that children are a product of genealogical roulette. That is certainly true of our brood. G. B., like me, has a strong sense of independence. He's a real iconoclast and has been antiestablishment ever since we remember. He definitely marches to the beat of his own drum.

In our family we have a joke: our middle son, Brad, is the "perfect" child. Of course, there is no such thing, but Brad certainly was a joy to raise. He moved west thirty-five years ago to attend the University of Denver, where he earned a bachelor's degree in business administration; after that, he earned a master's degree in architecture from the University of Colorado Denver. He's lived in Denver ever since (except for a period of three years in New York City, where he moved to be with Corey after she graduated from business school).

Brad lives with his wife, Marthe, in a wonderful area of Denver called Washington Park. They have a son, Eddie (named after his proud grandfather), and a daughter, Emma (our only granddaughter). Brad's career makes use of his many talents as an architect, a real estate broker, and a property developer. Much of his development work is in Grand Lake, Colorado, a town that sits 9,200 feet above sea level. There, he and Marthe have a second home, a perfect place to enjoy skiing in the winter as well as fishing and boating in the summer.

Our youngest, Corey, was never a "girly girl." Barbara always wanted to see her in pretty dresses, but Corey was happier in shorts, climbing trees with her brothers. I remember one year she was given a beautiful dollhouse by her grandparents. We were surprised that it never caught her interest. Rather it was Brad, with his early interest in architecture and building, who became fascinated by it.

In addition to being an enthusiastic athlete (gymnastics, ice skating, tennis, and field hockey), Corey loved to write. As a sophomore at the Middlesex School, she and her friends started a newspaper called the *John Door News*—which featured their write-ups on the inside of the stalls in the student bathroom. (Clearly, she has her father's sense of humor.) After receiving her bachelor's degree in religion and fine arts from the University of Vermont, and after a three-year sojourn in the media and tech world in San Francisco, she returned to the East Coast to earn her MBA at Harvard. At Harvard she became the editor in chief of *The Harbus*, the school's newspaper. She is currently the business curator for TED Conferences. She and her husband, Jim Sperber, live in Manhattan with their three boys, Leo, Sammy, and our youngest grandson, Oscar.

One of our favorite experiences is spending time with all our grandchildren on holidays. We are blessed to live in two places, Nantucket and Ocean Reef, that they absolutely love, enjoying the beach in both spots at the right time of year! We have also taken them on special trips to Hawaii, Antigua, and Anguilla. I hope we have been able to instill the love of travel we shared with our children in them as well.

All in all, I am obviously a very blessed man to be surrounded by Barbara, our children, and grandchildren, a family group I could never have dreamed of in my earlier years. They mean the world to me. And my greatest wish is that they will all find in their own families the love and fulfillment they have blessed me with.

Giving a graduation speech at University of Rochester (2010)

CHAPTER TWENTY

The Need to Fix Something

c. 2008-2016

B Y 2016, I HAD BEEN THE CHAIRMAN OF THE BOARD of trustees at the University of Rochester for eight years. It had been a very fulfilling experience, a real chance to give back to my alma mater, which was my first real home. But let me step back and reflect on an association and involvement that has meant so much to me.

Back in 1980, when I was at Lehman Brothers, I made a presentation before the university's investment committee about the benefits of making a bond portfolio part of the endowment. I reasoned that this strategy would produce around a 14 or 15 percent return for a minimum of ten years. The bonds would be rated at least AA, and many of them would be government securities.

At the time, I had a bond whiz working for me at Lehman, but you didn't have to be a genius to construct such a portfolio back in 1980–81. However, after making my presentation, I was told by the committee, in no uncertain terms, that it did not buy bonds and was not interested in my proposition.

I swore right then and there that if the committee was that *unintelligent*, I would never go back and get involved with the university. Even so, I broke my own promise a few years later, when I made a contribution to my twenty-fifth class reunion, in 1983.

As it turned out, the endowment performed very poorly in the eighties. In fact, by 1988 it had become an embarrassment. Dennis O'Brien, the president at the time, was determined to reverse its decline. Because he knew I had managed a number of pension plans and endowments over the course of my career, he came to New York several times to try to persuade me to join the board and take over as chair of the investment committee. He was so committed to the cause that I think he once said he wasn't going to leave my office until I agreed to take the position.

At that point, conditions were ripe for my two worst personality traits to come into play—the need to fix something and the willingness to change my mind. I finally told Dennis that *if* I accepted the position, I didn't want go through the normal process of being vetted first by the alumni council and then by the board.

He agreed.

In 1988, I joined the University of Rochester's board of trustees and became the chairman of the investment committee. In short order, with the help of the university's CFO, Dick Greene, and a staff member, Joyce Johnson, I reconstituted the committee membership, revamped the fund, then managed it for the following fifteen years. Some people are convinced I saved the endowment. But in reality, I'd say I just did the job in a professional manner and positioned the endowment so that it performed in line with those of its peer institutions.

In 2000, we hired one of the best investment managers in the business, Doug Phillips, who had been the treasurer at Williams College. He became the senior vice president in charge of the university's investments, and he's still there today. He has built up a highly effective staff, and the endowment is now among the best managed in our peer group.

By 2003, I felt I had put in my time and was finishing a fifteen-year run as a trustee. In fact, my tenure violated the two-term limit set by the school. The president of the university at the time, Thomas Jackson, whose efforts had resulted in great improvements to the school's academic capabilities and image, did not see eye to eye with me regarding the lack of emphasis on development. I believed this was the key to the school's future and constituted a significant missed opportunity. In any case, I decided that it was time to step down. It wasn't the first time I'd left a position when I disagreed with how things were being run. Had this policy served me well over the years? Yes and no. However, I always seemed to end up at a place where I could make a greater contribution.

I was proud of my accomplishments during my fifteen years on the board. In addition to managing the endowment, I chaired the campaign to rebuild our athletic facilities, which brought our basketball court up to regulation size. Subsequently our men's and women's teams started to regularly make the NCAA Division III "Sweet 16" playoffs. Build it and they will come—and win. I also set up a scholarship program for engineering majors and did quite a bit of work with the business school.

AS I MENTIONED, in 2004, the board decided it was going to do a search for a new president. Thomas Jackson had been in office for ten years, which was the usual term. A number of the senior trustees, including the chair, Bob Witmer, and the previous chair, Bob Goergen, asked me to return to the board "just for the presidential search."

I agreed to return to the board, but I made it clear that my commitment was for one year—two at the most.

Near the end of the search I became frustrated with the lack of progress and suggested that we pick the five best candidates and then arrange for five trustees, as a group, to interview each of them over a single forty-eight-hour period. To facilitate this process, I even agreed to provide a private plane to fly them to the interviewees' locations. Further, I said I did not have to be among that five-person group. The other trustees could use the plane to make the interviewing process easier and more efficient, as long as they picked a new president out of the five best candidates.

The group insisted I come along, so I agreed to go. The first person we met was Joel Seligman, who, as I mentioned, was the dean of Washington University School of Law, in St. Louis. I took an instant liking to Joel. During our interview, we asked him an exhaustive list of questions, and he answered them all brilliantly. We emphasized the need for development and communications—my hot-button issues—and he received the message loud and clear. He even commented on these issues before we brought them up. Toward the end, when I asked him what he did in his spare time, he almost blew the interview when he answered, "I read securities briefs."

No golf, no tennis, no fishing! Luckily, we chose to gloss over this weakness.

Joel turned out to be far and away our best choice. After we conducted the other interviews, he was offered the job.

Once the position of president had been filled in 2005, I wanted to return to civilian life. But the chair of the board of trustees at the time, Bob Witmer, who happened to be one of my old fraternity brothers, didn't want me to leave just yet. Nor did Joel, who said, "You're one of reasons I came to Rochester, so you've got to stay another year."

Yielding to their blandishments, I agreed. But after a year had gone by, and Joel was off to an excellent start, he invited me to that fateful dinner and asked me to become chairman of the board of trustees. Just when I thought I had both feet out the door, too.

In response, I wrote one of the best letters of my life, articulating the four reasons why making me chairman was not a good idea—and, frankly, why it was impossible.

First, I was too old. I was then seventy-two. The bylaws stated that seventy was the maximum age for someone in that position.

Second, I considered myself unable to give a transformational gift—meaning a gift large enough to really send a message to the alumni. I thought that the ability to give such a gift was a critical prerequisite for anyone taking the job, because that person would thereafter have to lead a comprehensive capital campaign.

Third, I lived hundreds of miles from Rochester and could not attend all the functions that a chair should attend. Barbara had agreed to "for better or for worse," but she didn't agree to live in Rochester.

And finally, why replace Bob Witmer? There was simply no comparison! He was by far the best man for the job. When we were in college, he was president of our fraternity, whereas I was the social chairman. He was Phi Beta Kappa, whereas I was not even Tau Beta Pi (though I eventually did make it in as one of the oldest members ever, in 2015). Bob was captain of the varsity basketball team and played an instrument in the band, whereas I was on the freshman basketball team (and had to give it up) and possessed no musical talent at all.

I thought I had squashed this absurd request once and for all when Joel came back yet again and said, "I'm a lawyer. I can fix the bylaws problem."

"Okay, but what about the Rochester thing and the Bob thing?" I asked.

That's when Bob called and said, "I'm finishing my five years, and it's now your turn, Ed." Clearly, Joel really wanted me to do it.

Foolishly, I asked Bob if he would agree to attend all the Rochester events that I would not be able to attend were I to accept the chairmanship. He readily said yes! In fact, he said it was something he would really like to do.

With three of my four reasons for declining eliminated, I went to talk to Jim Thompson, the head of development, whom I had become very fond of since his arrival. We sat down to discuss my part in a capital campaign and what was expected. Joel had asked for $10 million, but I felt if I were going to make a major impact and create a transformation at the university (why else take the job?) I had to give much more than that.

I asked the $30 million question: What was the largest gift ever given to the university?

Jim said that George Eastman had given $27 million in 1927.

I sat quietly for a moment. I thought if I could get to $30 million, *that* would send a message.

It was early 2008. Remember, I was getting bearish on the world. I was in the process of closing my hedge funds. And I started to feel that taking this job, and giving away a big chunk of my net worth, was the right thing to do—that it was somehow meant to be.

I called my family—some individually, but most of them together in a group—and talked about making the gift. Barbara immediately agreed, and our children quickly and unanimously said, "Go for it, Dad."

That was exactly the confirmation I needed and wanted to hear. After all, it was part of my family's inheritance: in a sense, it was their money, not mine, and I didn't want to make the gift if any of them strongly objected to it.

After a little more due diligence and quite a bit of introspection (listening to that inner voice), I finally accepted the position and was installed as chairman of the board in May of 2008. My gift was announced in October of that year as the largest single gift commitment in the university's 158-year history (in nominal dollars). I called it a Roger Bannister gift, after the first man to run a mile in less than four minutes, in the hope that my record would be quickly broken by many others. Unfortunately, it hasn't happened yet: six months after I made my gift, the financial crisis of 2008 ensued, and the economic consequences to many potential donors were devastating. But I know that the record will be broken someday.

As I said at the university's trustees dinner at the time of the gift, "higher education is the cornerstone of economic strength in our increasingly interconnected world. It will be even more important in the decades ahead, and our nation's foremost research universities will lead the way. A great tradition in this country is that we try our best to improve the world we inherited for the generations that will follow us. Supporting a vibrant center of innovation and discovery like the University of Rochester is simply the best way I can fulfill this obligation." To acknowledge my gift, the university decided to name the School of Engineering and Applied Sciences after me, which was a great honor. This not only allowed me to repay the school for my excellent education but also satisfied what I consider to be one of the major needs of our country—the education of more engineers and the expansion of educational opportunities in all areas of technology.

The majority of my donation went toward scholarships, which has been my primary area of philanthropic emphasis for more than thirty years. I have endowed scholarships at University of Rochester; Harvard Business School; the University of Denver; the University of Vermont; the University of California, San Diego; Brunswick School in Greenwich Connecticut; and Middlesex School in Concord, Massachusetts. At one time, there were twenty Hajim Scholars, as we call them, enrolled in the engineering school. It has been a great pleasure to interface with them on a regular basis.

I also helped bring a terrific new dean to the engineering school, Rob Clark, who had been the dean of the Pratt School of Engineering at Duke University and who did a great job increasing our engineering population. In 2018, there were 1,700 engineering students, up from 700 when he took over. As a result of his strong leadership and the excellent academic program, the freshman class at the University of Rochester is now one-third engineering majors.

In 2016, Rob was named the school's provost in recognition of his many accomplishments. With my strong support, his successor, Wendi Heinzelman, who holds a doctorate from MIT, became the engineering school's first female dean. This was a far cry from my undergraduate days, when there were no women, either professors or students, in the engineering department.

———————

ON MAY 8, 2016, I COMPLETED MY TERM as chairman of the board of trustees. During my eight years in the position, we raised more than $1.37 billion in the first comprehensive capital campaign undertaken since 1927.

Every metric of the university has improved: as of 2016, there are a record number of applications, all-time high SAT scores, and a record number of early decision applicants. We created more than one hundred new endowed professorships, provided $225 million for student scholarships, and created many new programs and majors. In addition, we put almost $900 million of concrete on the ground for new buildings and facilities, including the Golisano Children's Hospital, which is the largest project in the school's history since the completion of the River Campus in 1930.

It was a very productive eight years, and I believe we accomplished most, if not all, of our goals. Not least important, we greatly expanded our involvement in and contribution to the Rochester community. The most recent example of this is our university's "takeover" of East High School, the largest in the city, a public school that was in dire straits.

All this happened while I was chair, but all the credit should go to Joel Seligman, who truly created an inflection point in the trajectory of the school. He was tireless in his efforts to take the institution to the next level, and he did it. I believe he should go down as one of the most influential and successful presidents in the school's history.

At my final board meeting, to thank all the trustees, I presented each of them a triangular crystal paperweight, engraved with their name and the sign-off *Thanks, Ed*. I also gave each a copy of *This Is the Moment!*, a book by Walter Green about gratitude and giving. That afternoon was a poignant occasion for me, truly *my* moment.

As I look back on my own campus days in Rochester, I never could have imagined that all *this* would have happened! After all, I was the kid with a funny haircut and the beat-up leather jacket. I was on a scholarship. I had nothing—no family support and no money. I did have one important thing—the conviction that getting an education was the passport to a better future. But I certainly never thought I'd wind up having a school named after me or being chairman of the board! Not even in my wildest dreams.

Yet it only proves that everybody has a chance. Everybody is on the road to the next destination. We can all find a pathway forward, no matter what the situation. I'm very grateful to have had the chance to do it.

I must say that the university has been extremely laudatory of my efforts. In 2013, I was honored with the Dean's Medal, followed by the Eastman Medal in the spring of 2016. Also in October of 2016, the Engineering and Applied Sciences Quadrangle was dedicated in my name. This was truly an unbelievable honor, because the only other quad on campus is named for George Eastman.

To make the story even more like a fairy tale, Joel Seligman commissioned an eight-foot bronze statue of me that was placed in the quadrangle upon its completion. From black leather jacket to bronze statue in just sixty-two short years! Yes, I am the first one in my neighborhood to have a statue created in my honor. Thanks, Joel.

Receiving the Horatio Alger award with my sponsor, Patrick Lee (2015).

CHAPTER TWENTY-ONE

Coming Full Circle

c. 2015

IN 2015, I ASKED BARBARA WHAT SHE WANTED for her birthday.

"I want you *happier!*" she exclaimed.

Her statement took me by surprise. I will concede that I don't laugh as much as I should, and to most observers I appear to be a rather serious person. Perhaps it's because I didn't get to do a lot of the fun things that most kids get to do with their families. I do have a lot of friends, and have enjoyed my work and my athletic activities. Still, my difficult background stayed with me, lingering into adulthood as a subtext beneath everything: in my mind, I'm still just a street kid who went out into the world and tried to make something of himself.

But these days, in my eighties, I give myself much more credit than I used to. I can appreciate the efforts I've made and the ways in which I've been able to contribute. Having read the classic book *The Seasons of a Man's Life*, by Daniel J. Levinson, I see that I'm at the stage where I can finally *accept* myself to a much greater degree than I could before. This allows me to finally enjoy life a little more.

As my book began, I shared with you the day I was presented with the Horatio Alger Award. And I have to admit that this first public recognition of the path I had taken from childhood to adulthood was heartening.

In April of 2015, my friend and colleague Patrick Lee, a former aeronautical engineering major who went on to establish a successful international manufacturing business, recommended me for the prestigious award. As I explained, it's given to leaders who demonstrate a commitment to philanthropy and to higher education and who have overcome significant personal challenges to achieve success.

I first heard about the Horatio Alger Association of Distinguished Americans many years earlier. As I understood it, it was an organization that recognized people who started with nothing and went on to make significant contributions to society. Later, I discovered that its primary goal is to give scholarships to underprivileged kids. This I was truly interested in. It had been the main focus of my charitable giving for years. For that reason alone, the organization seemed like a perfect fit with my story—if only I could find the courage to share it publicly.

My hesitation became a moot point when Patrick's recommendation was accepted and I won the award. At that point, I had run out of excuses not to share my story.

THAT BRINGS US FULL CIRCLE to the day in Washington, DC, when I confronted the map on the wall of the Smithsonian, which put me back in time, allowing me to retrace my childhood journey. What a long way I had come—way more than the 1,800 miles between St. Louis and Los Angeles.

Receiving the Horatio Alger Award brought closure to my past. It allowed me to own my history and my experience. I was proud to be a living example of the fact that no matter how daunting or insurmountable your circumstances may appear, *anything is possible.*

It also gave me a forum in which to express my gratitude for everything I have been blessed with, especially Barbara and my family. I am also grateful to my family for never letting me drink my own whiskey, or get a big head.

And though I held my breath as the video about my life began to roll that night, I also let out a sigh of relief when I saw myself on the giant screen. Oddly, it felt good to let it all go.

I no longer have to hide my past. It's finally out in the open. When the two-minute clip ended and the room broke into applause, I could tell that people had been really touched by it, that they had listened and heard what I had to say. I was both overwhelmed by their reaction and relieved that it was over.

BARBARA WANTS ME TO SLOW DOWN, drink iced tea on the porch, and spend more time alone with her. I can't see that happening anytime soon, because I feel there's still so much to do. Yet maybe I've done just enough.

I haven't found the holy grail, and I haven't achieved every one of my goals. But I have experienced something almost as amazing: I've lived the American dream. Many think of it as a clichéd, outmoded concept. Believe me, it isn't. It's alive and well.

I believe today's young people have more opportunity than I had. Today, there are so many more possibilities in a wider variety of fields than there were in the 1950s and 1960s. The world now has a global communications network, instant access to the internet, and all modes of social media to bring us all together, no matter where we are. In a single keystroke, an entrepreneur can access the power of global commerce, adding billions of potential customers for any new business with no limits to geographical location.

For sure, start-ups can enter the marketplace with fewer obstacles than entrepreneurs faced in my generation. Likewise, fewer industries are entrenched in their positions. In addition, many new businesses don't need bricks and mortar to survive, as legions of them require only a small amount of capital to get off the ground. All these things make the American dream even more possible than it ever was before.

On the downside, the government is not as friendly to business as it was in my day, and a complicated web of regulations makes business more difficult to operate. These days, one also needs a higher level of education to compete for highly selective jobs. But given the expansion of opportunities, such challenges can be overcome. While some skeptics believe the young people of this generation won't do as well as their parents did, remember, skeptics said the same thing in 1990, just before the internet boom!

In some areas of life, things look particularly dark as I write this. And in the financial markets, I expect some very difficult times over the near term. But in my experience, upheaval sometimes presents major new opportunities.

This book is my attempt to capture my experience on the road less traveled, tracking my journey from being a vagrant, parentless child to a businessman with a large, loving family and the resources to help others accomplish their dreams. Isn't that all anyone could strive for?

I believe it was Giuseppe Verdi who said, "Now that I am eighty, my internal fires are out and therefore I can begin my life's work."

I don't believe in ever truly retiring from life. I guess my plan is to continue to do anything that intrigues me, productive pursuits that allow me to join forces with others who can help me leave the world a better place than it was when I found it. As for Barbara (who knows me all too well), when she hears the question "What's next?" she just laughs!

Here I am with the Hajim Scholars at the University of Rochester.

The Four *P*'s—Passion, Principles, Partners, and Plans

W hen I became chairman of the board of trustees at the University of Rochester, I thought I should have some sort of *story* I could share with students—a message that could be both motivating and inspiring.

For several years, I had been giving a speech about life planning to students at the university's Simon Business School. In addition, I spoke to members of the YPO and CEO.

At first, my speeches mostly focused on the importance of making strategic plans for the future. I always shared part of my story: as a high school student living in an orphanage, I dreamed of escaping that life, and that dream came true through dogged determination and planning.

However, the more I thought about it, the more I realized that these speeches didn't quite convey the whole message. I began to understand the importance of three other words that—in addition to *plan*—begin with *p*: *passion*, *principles*, and *partners*.

In my view of things, you must follow your *passion*, understand and live by your core *principles*, make appropriate *plans*, and choose the right *partners*. I felt these four *p*'s were all closely connected. And there's no doubt each played a large role in my success.

As I developed the "four *p*'s" concept, I began talking about it at graduations, convocations, and in private, anytime I mentored a young person who came to me seeking career advice. It's a memorable and simple composite of guideposts that seemed to quickly resonate with my listeners in a very personal way.

In the course of my dialogue with students, I have learned that their parents sometimes debate with them which of the four *p*'s they think is the most important and which most apply in their lives. The idea seems to resonate with people of all ages—from baby boomers to teenagers. That makes me think I might be on to something, so as this book comes to a close, and as part of my aim to contribute, I'd like to share my thoughts about each of these four vital concepts.

P NUMBER 1: PASSION

Passion is one of those words we all use, yet I find it is often misunderstood. For example, if someone had asked me what I was passionate about early in my career, I would have said, "Science and mathematics," which gradually morphed into engineering. Later in my career, I would have answered, "Money management." Still later, I would have said, "People management." Passion is a dynamic and ever-changing force that drives us forward in life.

When you feel truly passionate about any pursuit, it no longer even seems like work. Instead, the hours fly by because you're genuinely consumed, totally into what you're doing. Throughout my life, I've always had *something* that I couldn't wait to do, something I wanted to engage in every day. I still feel that way—even now, when most people my age are slowing down. Not me. I've written this book, which has engaged my attention for more than two years. And I'm still looking around the corner, wondering what I'll do next.

However, young people just starting out in their careers are often told, "Simply follow your passion, and the world will be your oyster." Putting that cliché aside, I've observed that many young people (engrossed in social media on their phones!) don't know *what* they're passionate about, let alone the differences between a passion, a dream, or even a pleasant activity. Sometimes I ask people what they're most passionate about, and they rattle off things I'd consider hobbies rather than career choices, such as tennis, golf, baseball, or some version of partying.

It can be challenging to discern what your true passion is if you're not accustomed to self-reflection or self-examination. It can also be difficult if you've been so busy you haven't had time to slow down and listen to your inner self. And that's difficult to do in the 24–7 news cycle, with a social media feed that never rests. It's easy to become compulsively distracted, which detracts from the ability to focus on your passion.

If you're unsure about what road to follow, ask yourself the following questions:

- What keeps me awake at night?
- What makes me take the stairs two at a time?
- What's the difference between my "should" and my "must"?
- If money weren't a factor, would I still want to do this?

———————————

Here's another way to find your passion: if you're a student, after the school year ends, use your summers. As you saw from my story, I took every opportunity I could for foreign travel, learning about various companies, cultures, and traditions, and finding great mentors along the way. Never waste a chance to test yourself in an unfamiliar environment. If you're willing to take a risk and throw yourself into a new opportunity (even when it's out of your comfort zone), you have a much better chance of finding your true calling.

Throughout my career, I could have made a lot more money by choosing positions based on pay alone. But I wanted freedom and the ability to immerse myself in companies that really interested me. At the same time, I wanted to create *balance* between my family and my professional life.

I often advise people—whether they're looking to enter the job market for the first time or making a career change later in life—that understanding *who you are* and *where you belong* is more important than making money. In my case, I looked for corporate positions in which I could make the biggest impact. As you'll recall, I chose to move to a small firm like Furman Selz rather than a much larger and more bureaucratic company. I chose the playing field where I could be the most effective leader, the place where I could make the biggest difference.

Guy Kawasaki's fascinating book *The Art of the Start* teaches a very powerful lesson on this subject. His advice is to go out into the world and *make meaning, not money.* This message became even more resonant with me as I matured in my career. It took time and experience to understand the real value of meaning over money. But once you choose passion over profit, and meaning over money, your life will change for the better, too. When you accomplish this, you will never have to "work" a day in your life.

———————

There are many skills in life that can be learned at a university, yes. But deep down, true passion is not taught or acquired—it is inherent. In the movie *The Legend of Bagger Vance*, about a down-on-his-luck golfer who enlists the help of a caddy named Bagger Vance, there is a scene in which Bagger says to the golfer, "Inside each and every one of us is one true authentic swing. Something we was born with. Something that's ours and ours alone. Something that can't be taught to you or learned. Something that's got to be remembered."

Real passion cannot be found *outside* yourself. And it can't be given to you by somebody else. It's cultivated through the books you read as a kid, the movies that inspired you, the teachers who helped you along the way, the friends you had, the jobs you loved—even the messy childhood you might have experienced.

In short, all great and committed passion comes from within. It is developed as we live.

P NUMBER 2: PRINCIPLES

Simply stated, principles are the rules you live by. Like discerning passions, developing your principles is a lifelong process. I've found that both my early religious training and the people I met along the way (whether in orphanages or at school) gave me many of the core principles I live by.

The Golden Rule

The single most important principle I live by was taught to me in Catholic schools: "Do unto others as you would have them do unto you." That concept, the Golden Rule, has guided and inspired me since childhood. It's so basic yet so meaningful.

When you're a boss and you treat other people as you want to be treated, two amazing things happen. First, your employees respect you because it reinforces their belief that you value them. Second, people you treat fairly will respond in kind. You get better overall cooperation from your team, which results in better performance.

In my corporate career, I never wanted to be fired. As a rule, therefore, I don't fire people unless I really *have* to. In fact, in my twenty years at Furman Selz, I only fired two people on the spot—one was doing drugs on the job and the other took a very large nonauthorized position that could have cost our company millions of dollars.

If someone you hired isn't working out, I believe at least half the problem is *yours*: either you hired the wrong person or you put that person in the wrong job. When that happens, and you have to let someone go, allow that person enough time to tie up loose ends, make alternative plans, and leave with dignity. Sometimes this route may not be the most economical choice for the company, but it sends a positive message to others: they're working for an employer who is good and fair.

We are all unique individuals with different needs and struggles. Each of us has the potential for growth and something of great value to offer if we're put into the right role that matches our abilities and passion. When you treat people with kindness and respect, chances are that those qualities will become evident quickly.

Set an Example for Others

People are always watching you.

They pay close attention to how you act and treat others both in the office and outside of it. So next time you're at the company holiday party or corporate retreat, remember that people are observing how you behave at all times.

You have the opportunity to set an example for others wherever you go—so you might as well set the bar high. Demonstrating what kind of person you are leaves absolutely no room for others to turn your words back on you. Show people who you are; don't just tell them.

Never Compromise Your Principles in Order to Be Accepted

We all want to belong, to be "one of the guys" or "one of the gals." This often requires conforming to what other people do. But there are times when you will need to stop, take a beat, and say, "That's a line I won't cross. I'm not going to do that."

What are the lines you won't cross?

Living by your stated principles is sometimes challenging. It's not that easy to set boundaries, to be clear and unapologetic about what you stand for. It's much easier to cave into peer pressure from others. But following the herd can lead to undesirable—and even devastating—consequences. When you compromise your principles, you're essentially lying to others and to yourself, and it can backfire and come back to haunt you. You need to stand up for yourself, even if it means not being accepted by the "in crowd." You may even alienate others whose help you might need in the future. But you have to draw that line somewhere.

The Human Touch

I like to show people that I genuinely care about them by paying attention to their lives outside the office. Over the years, I've gone out of my way to acknowledge major events in the lives of others, whether it's a wedding, birthday, anniversary, or baby shower. Whether it's for my administrative assistant, an IT worker I rarely see, or one of my traders, I will send a bottle of champagne or make a personal phone call or send flowers—whatever is appropriate. There is great value in letting people know you care.

When I send a card for a major occasion, I don't have a machine stamp my signature. I personally sign each one. It might take extra time, but people appreciate the gesture, and the truth is that I still get a kick out of doing it.

You never know what's going on in someone's life, but you can always count on a small gesture having a big impact.

If You Do Something for Someone, Don't Expect Anything in Return

Not everything in life is *reciprocal*. Give because you *want* to give, not because you're looking for something in return. If you do give conditionally, chances are that you may be disappointed. When you give to others, do it because it's worthwhile.

The more you give, the more you get. When I started to give of myself, my life changed. My experience was enriched in ways I could never have imagined. I derive my greatest satisfaction by watching others succeed because of the help I gave them. In fact, you will find that you can't really *give* anything away, because it always comes back, one way or another.

In his book *Give and Take: Why Helping Others Drives Our Success*, Adam Grant notes that there are three types of people—takers, matchers, and givers.

- *Takers*—They're always trying to get as much as possible from others.
- *Matchers*—If they do you a favor, they expect one back.
- *Givers*—They go out of their way to support and help you, with no strings attached.

Be a giver!

Give Credit More Often Than You Take It

The old saying "There's no *I* in team" never rings truer than when you are running a company or supervising a group of people in any type of organization. Regardless of my role, I always try to deflect success and not worry about who gets credit for a job well done. That's because the bottom line affects us all.

Own Your Mistakes

This principle is simple: if you did something that didn't work out, just own it! Make an immediate amend. Don't procrastinate. It's cleaner and faster to just own up to it.

Raise your hand and say, "Yup—it was me." People will respect you for your honesty and integrity. They'll also appreciate not having to take the blame for something they didn't do.

We learn just as much from failure as we do from success—probably more. In fact, I'd say failure is a necessity, a prerequisite for success. As one pundit wrote, "A credible failure makes an entrepreneur more investable." Why? Because you learn what doesn't work. It's like an athlete who practices a move over and over again, often falling or failing. But in the process, he finds out what works. Don't fear failure. Embrace it as a growth opportunity.

P NUMBER 3: PARTNERS

Proximity is the messenger of fate. In other words, our peer group—those whom we choose to associate with and come into contact with on a daily basis—very much determines the course of our lives. The people in our physical orbits—those in closest proximity—will often become the people most important to us.

When you're around someone in your environment, day after day, you notice their insight, humor, and unique talents—and the needs in them that call out to you for fulfillment. When we look to each other for companionship, love, and connection, we often get what we need. That's why I always say that the people you choose to bring into your life truly make a difference.

If you're like most of us, you need other people in your life to recognize and appreciate your worth, to reinforce your strengths, especially if you fail to see them in yourself, as I did for so long. Those are the people who lift you up and buoy you through uncertain and challenging times. They provide a perspective you may lack. They understand what you are truly capable of.

As I see it, the most important partner you have in this regard is your spouse. He or she will be there for you no matter what—and likewise, you will be there for him or her. Choose wisely. I know I did.

All my business accomplishments pale in comparison to the success I've achieved in my marriage and family. As you have read, Barbara is the best thing that has ever happened to me. She may not always be right, but trust me, she is rarely wrong. She's taught me the meaning of unconditional love, something she has selflessly given me for more than fifty years. She has also given me the family I always dreamed of. She has been my rock and remains my touchstone. I love her more than I did yesterday and less than I will tomorrow. Believe me, without Barbara, I wouldn't be where I am today. *That's* what makes her a tremendous partner.

Other than in marriage, too, there's tremendous value in surrounding yourself with people who either do things *better* than you do or who do things you don't want to do. Each partner brings different skills and assets to the table.

For example, I spent thirty-five years relying on one man to handle all the technical aspects of our businesses, including HR, IT, and accounting. I never once had to worry if things weren't being taken care of or if the financials were correct. Knowing he had these things covered made him a terrific partner. It allowed me to concentrate on the job I had to do. This is what partnership is all about.

Having grown up extremely independent, I took a long time to understand the significance of learning to trust and embrace my partners. You can't be a do-everything-yourself kind of person. I navigated through many tough times on my own and didn't believe I needed anyone else to help. But I did. And it was a tough lesson. There are people who think I still don't ask others for help often enough. But now I know how important it is to do so.

In the end, you are only as good as the people you surround yourself with.

P NUMBER 4: PLANS

Throughout our lives, we all should make plans, setting out for where we want to go and imagining what it will be like when we "arrive."

But what happens when life doesn't happen according to our plans? No matter how hard we try, we can't control how every plan works out. But we still do need strategic planning!

Even the simplest things in life—like getting from one destination to another—are not always easy to implement or accomplish without a strategy. That's where the fourth *p* comes in—planning.

Think of your plan as a personal GPS. You wouldn't go on a road trip without plotting your course, so why would you go through life, start a business, or launch your career without a plan?

You already have the first three *p*'s in place. You've answered the primary questions:

- What are your *passions*—the interests and ideas that energize you most?
- What are your *principles*—the fundamental precepts that guide your choices and actions?
- What are the characteristics of the *partners* you will seek in life and work?

Now it's time to ask yourself the final question: How will you combine your passions, partners, and principles to create an evolving plan of action for pursuing your dreams?

Planning is a step-by-step process. The more carefully you plan for the future, the more easily you can adapt to unexpected changes in the present; and the earlier you begin planning, the more effective and content you'll be in your career and life.

You may have heard a frequently repeated piece of advice in business circles: "If you don't know where you're going, any road will get you there."[8] I sometimes think whoever said it first was trying to encourage a younger person or a lost soul to get off his or her keister and take action. But the truth is that having a specific direction makes a huge positive difference: in my experience, your chances of satisfaction and happiness are much greater if you have a plan. No one knows what the future holds, and life has a way of taking us on a journey we can't anticipate. But if you're aiming at a goal, you will always be moving; you will never stagnate.

You also may have heard that writing your goals down increases your chances of success. That's true in my experience. In fact, in 2007, a professor at the Dominican University of California, Gail Matthews, conducted a study on the subject and found that people who write their goals down are 42 percent more likely to achieve them than people who don't write them down. It's simply more evidence that planning works.

EMO: Environment, Me, Opportunity

When you're making a plan, there are certain elements that have to come together—some of which are under your control and some of which aren't. A good plan recognizes these factors and allows for the unexpected. Your understanding of them strongly influences your success.

---

[8] This is actually a paraphrase of a conversation from *Alice in Wonderland* between Alice and the Cheshire Cat:
"Would you tell me, please, which way I ought to go from here?"
"That depends a good deal on where you want to get to," said the Cat.
"I don't much care where—" said Alice.
"Then it doesn't matter which way you go," said the Cat.
"—so long as I get SOMEWHERE," Alice added as an explanation.
"Oh, you're sure to do that," said the Cat, "if you only walk long enough."

I refer to these as the "EMO" factors: *E* stands for "environment," *M* stands for "me," and *O* stands for "opportunity." It's the interplay among them that helps you determine a course of action.

The environment is essentially your circumstances—what's going on in the world at the moment you need to make a decision. Is China going to be the next business behemoth? Are plastics—to hark back to *The Graduate*—going to be the next big consumer commodity? Is the market for recreational vehicles going to double or triple in five years?

Next, examine yourself—your "me." What are your talents? Are you good at working behind the scenes? Are you a good communicator? And, of course, what are your passions? Do any of these things merge with what you see in the environment?

Finally, recognize opportunity when it comes along. You can't force an opportunity to come to you, but you can open the door when it knocks.

Asking the Right Questions

As you develop your plan of action, ask yourself the following questions:

- **What's my vision?** Your vision is your dream—your ultimate hope for the future—and defining it is the first step in making a plan. For help in identifying it, go back to thinking about what your passions are. Use some of the same techniques to clarify your vision. Think about the EMO factors: What's truly *me*? What fits with who I am at my core?
- **What will the environment be during my lifetime?** This also considers the EMO factors. Take the temperature of the air around you: do you spot any warming or cooling trends? Do you see any stormy weather on the horizon? Then do some research—what do other people see on the horizon?
- **What are the available paths to achieving my vision?** Let's return to the GPS metaphor. If you're going from point A to point B, your map software will tell you how to get there in

stages. For example, you have to get to Maple Street before you can turn right on Elm Street. Getting to Maple Street is your short-term goal; getting to Elm Street is your long-term goal.

Similarly, the path to achieving your vision consists of short-term and long-term goals. Short-term goals are clear and foreseeable objectives. Long-term goals may require more flexibility on your part because circumstances are likely to change along the way—for example, by the time you get to Elm Street, it might be closed to traffic because of a water main break. So you have to devise a different route.

Make a list of short-term and long-term goals, then establish deadlines that will help you stay the course. Do more research: are there any other ways to get to Elm Street? How have people gotten there in the past?

- **What am I willing to sacrifice to achieve my vision?** Sometimes taking a particular path means that you have to give something up. You might need to let go of something, whether it's an object or an idea. You might have to give up a habit or something that's been comfortable for you. You might need to rethink your partners and your principles. Imagine having to lose something you cherish in order to achieve your vision. What would that feel like? Great success sometimes entails great sacrifice, and it's important to know what you'll do—and won't do—to succeed.

At the end of each year, during the holidays, my family and I like to take a vacation together, usually at sea. As you read earlier, it's an opportunity for Barbara and me to be with our children and grandchildren for an extended period of time. I also use this getaway as an occasion to reflect on the previous year and make a blueprint for the coming year. I find being near the ocean is peaceful and tranquil, the perfect atmosphere for contemplation.

As I look back on the previous year, I always review my plan. What did I accomplish? What *didn't* I accomplish? I don't exactly keep score, but I like to know which of my goals were met and which ones I missed. I think about which objectives I'd like to carry over to the following year and which ones no longer feel important.

Whether you take stock of your goals at the end of the year or at some other point, it's a good idea to check in with yourself regularly. Plans will evolve—and so will you.

I believe in self-direction, self-discipline, hard work, and our country. In fact, I find it hard to comprehend that there are some who no longer think that capitalism is the best and fairest economic system and political philosophy in the world—one that ensures the greatest good for the greatest number of people.

All this is to say that a simple system like my four *p*'s philosophy isn't going to save the world on its own. But it might help people stay on track, discover what they most want to do in life, and attain it. My greatest hope is that the four *p*'s might enable you to fulfill your true potential, and thereby help others around you.

I offer the four *p*'s as guideposts that have helped me move forward and fulfill dreams that I thought were impossible. I hope they will do the same for you!

ABOUT THE AUTHOR

Edmund "Ed'" Hajim, the son of a Syrian immigrant, is a seasoned Wall Street executive with more than fifty years of investment experience. Born in 1936 in Los Angeles, he earned a BS in chemical engineering from the University of Rochester and an MBA with distinction from Harvard Business School. He thereafter held senior management positions with the Capital Group, E. F. Hutton, and Lehman Brothers before becoming chairman and CEO of Furman Selz. He has been the cochairman of ING Barings, Americas Region; chairman and CEO of ING Aeltus Group and ING Furman Selz Asset Management; and chairman and CEO of MLH Capital. In 2009, he became president of Diker Management and is now the nonexecutive chairman at HighVista Strategies.

In 2008, after twenty years as a trustee of the University of Rochester, Hajim began an eight-year tenure as chairman of the university's board. Upon assuming that office he gave the school $30 million—the largest single donation in its history—to support scholarships and endow the Edmund A. Hajim School of Engineering and Applied Sciences.

Through the Hajim Family Foundation, he has made generous donations to organizations that promote education, health care, arts, culture, and conservation. In 2015, he received the Horatio Alger Award, given to Americans who exemplify the values of initiative, leadership, and commitment to excellence and who have succeeded despite personal adversities.

The father of three children and grandfather to eight, Hajim and his wife, Barbara, split their time between Key Largo, Florida, and Nantucket, Massachusetts.